Invitation to
SOCIAL WORK

INVITATION SERIES

Invitation to Economics	David Whynes
Invitation to Linguistics	Richard Hudson
Invitation to Politics	Michael Laver
Invitation to Social Work	Bill Jordan
Invitation to Statistics	Gavin Kennedy

Other titles in preparation

Invitation to Archaeology	Philip Rahtz
Invitation to Engineering	Eric Laithwaite
Invitation to Law	William Twining
Invitation to Nursing	June Clark
Invitation to Philosophy	Martin Hollis
Invitation to the Sciences	Barry Barnes

Invitation to
SOCIAL WORK

Bill Jordan

BASIL BLACKWELL · OXFORD and NEW YORK

First published in 1984 by
Martin Robertson & Company Ltd.
Reprinted in 1985 by Basil Blackwell Ltd.,
108 Cowley Road, Oxford OX4 1JF.

Basil Blackwell Inc.
432 Park Avenue South, Suite 1505,
New York, NY 10016, USA

British Library Cataloguing in Publication Data

Jordan, Bill, 1941–
    Invitation to social work.
    1. Social work as a profession
    I. Title
    361′ .0023   HV10.5

ISBN 0-631-14235-5

Typeset by Katerprint Co Ltd, Oxford
Printed and bound in Great Britain by
T. J. Press Ltd., Padstow

Contents

	Acknowledgements	vi
	Preface	vii
1	Social Work and Social Workers	1

PART I   THE PERFECT FRIEND

| 2 | Good Advice | 31 |
| 3 | Wise Counselling | 45 |

PART II   THE SOCIAL SERVANT

| 4 | The Post-War Reformation | 67 |
| 5 | Reorganization and its Discontents | 81 |

PART III   THE POLITICAL ANIMAL

| 6 | Agitators and Agents of Control | 109 |
| 7 | Social Work and the Post-Industrial Society | 132 |

PART IV   CONCLUSIONS

8	Social Work in Action	151
	Postscript	186
	Further Reading	190
	Index	194

Acknowledgements

I would like to thank Katherine Peacocke, Bill Forsythe, Barbara Kahan, Michael Hay and Bob Holman for their helpful comments on and criticisms of early drafts of the book. I am also very grateful to Alex Allan, both for making this possible by producing a typed first draft, and for her immaculate production of the final typescript.

Preface

A well-phrased invitation should make the prospective visitor feel interested and excited about what he is to attend. It should also allow him to prepare himself realistically for the occasion – for instance, by advice about how to dress and what to bring with him.

Most people picking up this book will already have some ideas about social work. It was tempting to start from the conventional views of it which I encounter frequently, either in newspapers or in conversations. But this would be to phrase the invitation in a rather defensive way ('this is not what you think', or 'despite rumours to the contrary'), or to make it somewhat impersonal. Instead, I have tried to write it in such a way as to reflect my personal views and experiences in social work – to make it a personal invitation.

Despite occasional cynicism or even despair, my perspective is essentially that of an insider in social work practice, who has remained an enthusiast. After a year in what might euphemistically be called residential work (as an officer in a borstal) I did my training, and then practised as a probation officer for five years. Since then I have taught on a training course, while continuing to do a substantial amount of part-time work, first as a probation officer and for the past eight years in the psychiatric field. I have also, in the course of my present job, done a good deal of work with children and families, including work with statutory responsibilities (care and supervision orders).

I have found being a social worker rewarding and exciting.

It has confirmed my expectation that it would be difficult, and would force me to develop capacities that might otherwise have remained dormant. The reader should therefore be warned that, even when I seem to be describing social work from a position of detachment – even aloofness – this is not the case. I believe that social work can and should be done well, that it can be intelligently discussed and learnt about, and that it offers important clues about how society might be improved and developed. Thus, even when I seem to be most critical of social work and social workers, I am in fact committed to it as a positive and valuable activity.

On the other hand, I do not want to convey the impression that social work is a peaceful or conflict-free activity, or that there are agreed and well-tried formulae for doing it well. On the contrary, few aspects of its practice are solidly established, and its principles are constantly the subject of strife. I shall argue that this is because social work attempts to put into operation certain ideas about personal, social and political relationships in society. It is therefore open to dispute from anyone with new or critical ideas about any one of these aspects of human relations. This is its fascination – that it requires something of the wider vision and negotiating skills of the politician, as well as the detailed, intense and intuitive empathy of the personal counsellor. While these polarities can never be perfectly combined, the tension created by the attempt to achieve such a fusion constitutes part of the excitement of an invitation to social work.

1

Social Work and Social Workers

An invitation to social work is not quite like an invitation to one of the established academic disciplines, such as economics or politics. It is not even quite like an invitation to one of the newer social sciences, such as sociology or psychology. Although all of these subjects contribute to the theoretical knowledge which social workers need to practise well, none in itself constitutes a sufficient basis. Indeed, social work is a very practical activity, in which the personal qualities of the worker may be as important as the knowledge he or she possesses; in which *how* the worker acts and communicates may be as significant as what he or she decides to do; and the success or failure of which can be evaluated from several different perspectives.

The same could perhaps be said of a number of different professional or semi-professional activities. Even in medicine or the law, the importance of the political and social context of the transaction between professional and client, and of skill and sensitivity in communication, are coming to be recognized. But social work has perhaps more in common with nursing and teaching than with these 'ancient professions'. Soical workers do not command high status, either as possessors of exclusive scientific or legal expertise, nor as independent and autonomous decision-makers. They tend to be employed in large organizations, usually by local authorities, and thus to be answerable, through hierarchies of professional and administrative superiors, to elected committee members.

Yet social workers do have to make important decisions that have major effects on people's lives – sometimes in matters of life and death – and often they have to act alone, without the immediate support of their colleagues, or senior members of their organizations. Alternatively, other social workers – especially in residential homes – have to look after groups of people who have been judged too disturbed, disruptive and difficult to remain in their families, neighbourhoods or schools, and for whom other professionals have failed to make satisfactory arrangements. Even though these workers do have the support of each other, they are often isolated from other forms of assistance. Hence, although social workers do not have a great deal of power and status compared with other professions, they do have a good deal of responsibility in some of the most difficult issues which confront modern societies; and the public have (as media publicity of scandals reveals) high expectations of what they should achieve.

Consider the following short examples of the kinds of situations which face social workers every day:

(1) A thirteen year-old girl has been refusing to go to school. She is unhappy at home, where the situation between her parents is tense and violent; but she will not contemplate leaving home voluntarily, and her parents will not support any alternative arrangements for her education. A social worker from the local authority must try to negotiate with the girl, the family and the education authorities to find some solution to the problem of her need both for schooling and for some relief from the family tensions. If the social worker fails, then a decision must be reached, with the education authorities, and with legal advice, about whether to apply to the court for a care order. If such an order is granted, the girl will probably go to an assessment centre. There residential social workers will try to deal with her distress at being removed from home against her will, to get to know her in a strange environment, and to help her plan for her future educational and living arrangements. The first social worker must continue to work with her angry parents, and help retain their

links with her, as well as possible. What is the future for this girl?

(2) A man in his thirties is referred to a social worker by a psychiatrist. Previously he has been seen by his general practitioner and by a neurological specialist for a sudden onset of 'blackouts'. The man is a driver by occupation, and cannot work while he has this condition. A number of tests have been done, but none of them have revealed any physical abnormalities. The psychiatrist has prescribed traquillizers, but can offer no further psychotherapy, and the man's condition is not serious enough to warrant hospitalization. The man is angry to be referred to a social worker – what can she do that all these eminent doctors and specialists could not achieve? She finds out, after politely enduring his resentful questioning of her credentials, that he is still in the emotional aftermath of a painful divorce, and still very strongly attached to his ex-wife and children. However, he is living with a younger woman, who loves him, but whom he says he does not love. The social worker visits to discuss the situation with them, and finds a difficult and tense relationship full of emotional pain on both sides. Can the social worker help both parties plan their future? If she can, will this relieve the man's symptoms?

(3) A young couple come to the social services department for help. The man has just been made redundant, and has used his holiday pay from work to meet a debt. He did not realize that this holiday pay is counted at his income for the next two weeks by supplementary benefits, so he is not entitled to any money from that source. Because he previously had a long period of unemployment, he has not made sufficient National Insurance contributions to qualify for unemployment benefit; nor does he qualify for any redundancy payment. The couple already have rent arrears on their council flat, and a number of other debts. They are under threat of having their electricity and gas disconnected. They have two young children and they are penniless. The social worker must try to help them disentangle their relationships with a number of powerful agencies – the social security department, the housing department

and the fuel boards. He must advocate for them, negotiate on their behalf, or advise them on how to claim, appeal or ask for special consideration. He must also decide what material help his own department should offer, and discuss and advocate within his own organization over any resources which he considers the family should be offered.

(4) A health visitor refers a couple to the social services department. The couple have just had a baby, and the wife has told the health visitor that her husband, who has been twice married before, has been the father of three previous children, all of whom died in suspicious circumstances. Two of these deaths occurred while he was in the navy, and a third in his home town, 100 miles away. The woman, who is of fairly low intelligence, is vague about the details, and does not seem afraid of her husband, but the health visitor is very anxious. The social worker must make urgent enquiries, both from the naval welfare authorities, and in the man's home town. Eventually the replies he receives are negative; only one child died, and the man was away at sea when this occurred. The social worker has visited with the health visitor during the delay while the enquiries were being made. The man is both intimidating and, in his opinion, potentially violent, even though the child is being well cared for and the wife shows no fear of him. What should the social worker (and his senior) do next? Should they try to discuss things with the couple, call a meeting of all the professionals involved, or withdraw from the case?

(5) The home help organizer of a social services department refers an elderly lady to the social work team. The lady is complaining that her son, in whose flat she is living, is locking her in and stealing her money. The home help who calls seldom sees the son, because he is working away. The social worker calls, and finds that the old lady is very isolated, and her resentment against her son seems irrational. She meets the son, who is concerned about his mother, but can do no more for her because of work commitments. What should the social worker decide to offer? The department has day care facilities which would reduce the old lady's isolation, but

might provide only a short-term solution. Alternatively, should she encourage the old lady to get her name down on the waiting list for residential care in an old people's home? How will she react to the suggestion? Will she see it as a further threat, and be resentful, or will she regard it as a welcome opportunity to get some companionship and more physical care?

DILEMMAS OF SOCIAL WORK

These examples give some clues as to what sorts of things social workers do, and what special problems their activities raise for them in everyday practice. At one level, these problems are very practical, immediate, and particular to each individual client. What advice does this person need? What resources would help her solve her problems? Whose responsibility should this be? But at another level the problems are much more general, for each of these particular cases raises fundamental issues about the sort of society we are living in, and the role of social work, and of the social services of the 'welfare state'.

This is not surprising when we consider the structural position of social work in modern societies, and particularly in the advanced industrialized countries of the capitalist world. Whereas before the Second World War most social work was either done by volunteers or for voluntary (charitable) organizations, nowadays it is mainly an integral part of the state's social services. But for the most part social work can best be seen as a special *way* of giving certain social services, which it is difficult to give in other ways. This is why, in spite of important differences within structures, policy and administration, social work services tend to concentrate on the same types of human problems in quite contrasting societies.

Since the Second World War, all the major advanced industrialized countries (with the exception of Japan, though even its pattern is becoming somewhat more similar) have developed systems for social security, state provision of housing, health services, and state education. Proportions of national incomes spent on these services vary (for instance, the USA spends much less on state health and housing systems than Western European, British or Scandinavian countries, but more than most on education), but all gave considerable priority to the development of these social services in the 1950s and 1960s, and all in turn have questioned whether this priority could be maintained in the 1970s and 1980s. At the same time, state social work services were created or expanded in all these countries, and although the relationship between the major services and the social work agencies differed considerably in different nations, some common themes are universal. For instance, even where social workers are not directly attached to public welfare agencies which provide financial assistance (as they are, for instance, in the USA, in many continental countries and in Australia and New Zealand), they cannot avoid involvement in the whole business of poor people getting sufficient benefits to live on – by having to advocate or negotiate for them, if not to provide benefits or assess needs. Equally, whether they are attached to education, justice or public welfare departments, or whether they are part of a free-standing social work department (as they are in Britain) they cannot avoid involvement in issues about child neglect and abuse, and about juvenile delinquency and its appropriate 'treatment'. Whether or not they work directly for health departments, and whether or not they have to 'take orders' directly from doctors, they tend to be concerned with issues of child health, disability and handicap and the care of the elderly; and also with the welfare of patients in mental and general hospitals. Whether probation services are separate departments (as they are in England and Wales) or part of the major local authority social work service (as in Scotland), there will be some people with social work training involved in the work of the criminal courts and the divorce courts; and with providing a welfare service in prisons. And whether voluntary agencies continue to play an inportant role (as they do in many predominantly Catholic countries) or whether the state has a virtual monopoly of social services, the problems of relationships between the state (as represented by the courts and the other major services) and informal, neighbourhood and community organizations, and between the state and its citizens, are of central concern for social workers.

In other words, many of the duties of social workers seem to stem logically and directly from the social and economic structures of modern societies. The major social services represent the commitment of the state to meeting certain needs in a certain way – though there is much dispute between theorists about why exactly this has occurred, and in whose interests these services are provided. Social work in turn tends to be concerned with the kinds of tasks which require detailed and personal attention of a less specialized kind, and with people who, for whatever reason, do not seem to 'get by' on the standard ration of health care, education, housing provision or social security benefits which is available. Either they have special difficulties, or they reject what is offered, or they just do not 'fit in' with the systems that are supposed to meet their needs.

These universal features of social work services in the advanced capitalist countries have led some theorists to argue that social work can only be properly understood as a direct product of the social and economic structures of these nations. Many such theorists have pointed out that as state employees in such societies, most social workers have clear legal duties to keep under control certain sections of the population which are seen as potentially subversive or threatening to the interests of the ruling class. Thus for instance social workers are disproportionately concerned with the poor, the unemployed, the homeless, residents of deprived areas, and other socially disadvantaged groups. Social workers may seem to be offering them help and some limited material assistance, but much of what they do can be seen as keeping them 'in their place'; ensuring that they do not come to expect or demand more than the state is willing to give them, or undermine the smooth functioning of economic and social life. Similarly, social workers are universally involved with such 'deviant' behaviour as child abuse, delinquency, crime and mental illness, which threatens the status quo, and expresses notions of rebellion, unorthodoxy or protest which the ruling class wishes to suppress. Again, while social workers may seem to be softening the impact of traditional ways of dealing with 'deviants' – punishments, removals from the community to special institutions, physical coercions – closer examination reveals that these methods are still widely used, and in some cases even practised by social workers themselves (for instance, punishments, isolations and occasional violence in children's homes). Finally, even services which seem to be unequivocally 'helpful', and almost universally welcomed by their recipients (such as home help services and other forms of domiciliary and day care for the elderly) are revealed as being very strictly rationed, and even where more generously given, as perhaps contributing to the 'legitimation' (i.e. making more politically acceptable) of regimes which consolidate the power of the wealthy and systematically deny the claims of the poor.

These views of social work (which with modifications apply also to most of the other social services), must be taken seriously, and will be examined in the course of this book. They are not confined to academics and radical critics of social work; they correspond with the views and experiences of many social workers who practise, particularly in deprived city areas, in many parts of the capitalist world. It is worth pointing out too that they find an echoing response in the perceptions of social workers in many communist countries, where despite public ownership of the means of production and central economic and social planning, social workers are still disproportionately concerned with the poor and with 'deviants' (though not necessarily with deviant actions of the same kind, or with subversive ideas which are identical), and where also social services are seen as legitimating their political regimes.

Some social workers, indeed, come into social work with precisely these perceptions of the societies in which they live. In Britain, for instance, a strong political motivation and analysis of social problems is one recognizable background to entry into social work, whether at the level of local authority fieldworker, or in the residential sphere. But many other people who enter social work consider their clients' problems from a quite different perspective. Research has suggested that the majority of social work recruits are still primarily motivated by a religious or humanitarian concern for under-privileged or disadvantaged members of society. This motivation might well allow an equally strong perception of clients as 'unfortunates' or even 'victims'; but the overall context or framework in which religious or humanitarian entrants to social work would evaluate actions, feelings and decisions in human relations would be moral rather than political. This apparent clash between the moral and the political dimensions of social work will be one of the themes of this book.

We might also distinguish a third element in the motivation and background of potential social workers. This could be loosely classified as the 'social' – not so much a 'social conscience', which would be nearer to the religious motive, but more a social *awareness*. Such an awareness might include an acknowledgement of the impact of social and psychologi-cal factors on *all* human behaviour, a recognition of the importance of the social services as aspects of modern life, and a consciousness of the career opportunities opened up by the expansion of the social work agencies which has occurred in recent years. This 'social' element is less obviously at odds with either of the two other major traditions of social work, but it is distinguishable and important. It might be suggested that it is increasingly common amongst realistic entrants into social work occupations, especially in lower-status, less well-paid posts in residential, day-care and domiciliary services – home helps, care assistants in old people's homes, nursery workers, residential child care workers, and day-care assis-tants.

It has also been suggested – for instance by Geoffrey Pearson – that this 'social' element tends to predominate in the training that is offered for social work. Colleges and training centres tend to emphasize the 'consensus' elements in social work, and those aspects of the work and the clients' problems which can best be explained in terms of such 'neutral' social sciences as psychology and sociology. It also tends to present the social services in terms of their structure and administration, rather than the moral and political dilemmas which underlie their policies, and social work practice in terms of technical skills which can be learned and applied in any context, irrespective of the practitioner's moral and political views. This tends, it is argued, to present social work as far more scientific and technical than most full-time practitioners feel it to be, and to drain it of the very ethical and political content which has motivated most of its recruits.

Whether or not this is an accurate picture of how British social work courses have been run in the past, it seems unlikely that these underlying issues can be suppressed in the future, as the continued effects of scarce resources and pressing needs make their presence felt in the 1980s. Therefore in this book I have tried to do justice to all three of these elements – the moral, the social and the political – and to see whether they can be reconciled in practice.

SOCIAL WORK IN BRITAIN

It may at this point be helpful to give a very simple and schematic account of British social work agencies and their staffing. This makes no claim to being exhaustive, and makes no allowances for local variations. The system in England and Wales is described – the Scottish system is slightly different.

Local authority social services departments

These are the largest employers of social work staff, and have responsibility, among other things, for:

(1) *Residential and domiciliary services for the elderly and handicapped:* old people's homes, adult training centres, day centres, hostels for the handicapped, home helps, aids and adaptations, etc.

(2) *Child care services:* fieldwork, including preventive work

with families; investigation of alleged child abuse and neglect; reports to courts on cases concerning children's welfare and children 'beyond control' or 'in need of care and control'; day nurseries and other day-care services; children's homes, assessment centres and 'community schools' for children (mainly delinquents) requiring residential education and training outside the mainstream educational system.

(3) *Social work services in general and psychiatric hospitals:* after-care hostels, day centres.

(4) *General welfare responsibilities:* to provide advice and guidance on a range of social problems, especially children, mental illness and handicap, and disability.

Social services departments staff consist mainly of:

(1) *Managers, administrators and advisers:* most (but not all) of whom have a professional social work background and/or training. Some of these are found in local offices, many others are concentrated in 'headquarters' buildings and offices.

(2) *Field social workers:* most of whom are now professionally trained who are mainly responsible for assessing needs and co-ordinating work with clients living in the community, and with planning and co-ordinating day-care and residential services.

(3) *Residential and day-care social workers:* very few of whom are professionally trained, some of whom are predominantly concerned with the emotional care of clients (e.g. residential child care officers in children's homes, assessment centres, community schools and workers in family centres), but many others of whom are predominantly concerned with the physical care of their clients (e.g. care assistants in old people's homes).

(4) *Domiciliary workers:* home helps, family aides, mainly involved with practical tasks of care for vulnerable people living in the community.

The probation service
This is a separate service in England and Wales, and comes

11

under the Home Office rather than the Department of Health and Social Security. Its main duties are:

(1) Providing reports to the criminal courts, and supervising offenders placed on probation.

(2) The co-ordination of community service order schemes, day training centres, residential hostels, and other special facilities for offenders outside the prison system.

(3) Prison welfare and after-care, parole supervision.

(4) Providing reports for the divorce courts, and supervising children in cases concerning disputed custody or access.

The great majority of mainstream probation officers are professionally trained, though many community service organizers and residential workers are not.

Voluntary agencies

A large number of specialized voluntary agencies employ social workers in tasks which are broadly similar to those in the state sector. Some of these agencies provide more intensive work with groups already dealt with by the state agencies – for example, the Family Service Units with 'problem families', Barnardo's and the National Children's Homes with children – but others provide field and residential services for groups notoriously neglected by the state agencies, for example, the Cyrenians with single homeless people. There are also agencies or branches of voluntary organizations which specialize by method, such as group work, 'intermediate treatment' (including short-term, intensive residential work for adolescents) and family therapy (psychotherapy aimed at changing the functioning of whole families by working with them as groups). Finally there are self-help groups and community associations.

This list should make one paradox immediately evident. With the exception of some of the voluntary agencies, most social work organizations are fairly large and hierarchically structured, and most concerned with the direct implementation of state social policies – either through the provision of certain kinds of legally defined services, or through the control of certain legally proscribed behaviour. So there is an inbuilt tension in social work between the *personal* nature of the tasks and the fairly *impersonal* nature of their organizational and legal frameworks. On the one hand, there would be little point in employing social workers, rather than clerks or administrators, to do these tasks unless they had opportunities to assess their clients' individual needs and scope for dealing with them differently, according to their emotional problems; on the other hand, these services cannot be exclusively related to such individual priorities, otherwise their location in these organizations and legal structures would be counter-productive. Is becoming a social worker primarily to be understood in terms of the 'helping', 'caring' or 'therapeutic' content of the job, or according to the official, bureaucratic, legal and even potentially coercive powers and responsibilities it entails?

HELPER OR OFFICIAL?

There is no easy answer to this question, and it uncovers a tension which is present in every social worker's daily life. The truth is that – unless they are working in some very protected or specialized corner of the field – social workers neglect either side of their job to their peril.

To be effective, social workers in every branch of the work – fieldwork, day care, residential work or neighbourhood community work – need to be able to *understand* people's situations, and to *communicate* this understanding. It has often been pointed out that this understanding and communication is in many ways more like an art than a science. While theory and knowledge from the social sciences may help greatly in giving social workers insights into areas of human behaviour and culture with which they have no personal acquaintance, this form of understanding depends considerably on social workers' ability to use their imagination and intuition, and to perceive the common ground between their own feelings and experiences and those of their clients. A flat, prosaic, jargon-ridden response to a client's account of his problems may indicate that the social worker has read some books on the subject, but is unlikely to give the client any real sense of *being understood*, whether his difficulty is a complex and intimate emotional one, or arises from dealing with a large and powerful organization. To be effective, to make relationships with clients which will allow him to 'get alongside' them, and overcome their fear and mistrust, the social worker usually needs to be able to demonstrate in words, gestures and actions that he has an all-round appreciation of the client's particular circumstances and point of view.

This requires a very disciplined approach to the tasks of listening, formulating ideas, checking perceptions, making plans, consulting with clients about aims and methods, and working towards goals. It means that the social worker has to be able to distinguish accurately between the client's subjective perceptions and feelings and his own, and to see when the former are influencing the latter. It also requires him to be able to recognize in his own (sometimes uncharacteristic or surprising) reactions to clients or to situations, important indications of stresses in the client's world – including danger signals. None of this means tht social workers should not be 'emotionally involved' in their work; but it does mean that they should make a particular kind of use of themselves and their feelings in their relationships with their clients, which has to be learnt and constantly improved if good standards of practice are to be reached.

All this implies that social workers need to spend time with each individual client, group or neighbourhood, and take their different and sometimes conflicting needs seriously. It implies that they cannot be effective if they give people 'standard rations' of time and attention, or standard answers to problems. If people were exactly like each other, then there would be little point in a service which offered them personal attention, and which tried to discriminate between their needs. On the other hand, state social work agencies in particular are certainly not there solely to meet individual needs. On the contrary, they are explicitly charged with duties to require individuals to conform with legally-defined expectations, and to provide services according to politically-defined standards. Thus although the social worker is supposed to take each client seriously as an individual, he is supposed to balance this individual's needs against those of others competing for his attention and the department's resources, or against the conflicting needs of others in his family or neighbourhood who may be adversely affected by his behaviour.

Furthermore, as well as having to implement legal requirements, state social work agencies have to try to discover ways of working which can be shown *generally* to promote the welfare of the community, or bring about results (such as reductions of children in custody, or in admissions to mental hospitals) which are regarded as desirable for clients. This requires having *policies* – approaches to the tasks of assessment and help which reflect past experience and theoretical knowledge, based on research. This in turn means a particular division of labour, and combinations of social workers into teams, and specialization (by problem focus, area or method) which allow these approaches to be applied. All this tends to cut across a purely individual and *ad hoc* approach, and to reduce social workers' discretion and control over their jobs. It may or may not increase the amount of his work that is official, and where he is representing the agency in ways he would not necessarily choose to represent himself; but it will certainly mean that he cannot pose as being simply a free-wheeling helper or therapist.

What I have said about the discipline of helping and the constraints of policies and the legal framework should make it clear that social work is certainly not an activity in which people 'do their own thing' or just go around 'being themselves'. It also involves many of the contradictions to be found in other jobs in the public services, and in the private sector. People who come into social work anticipating an atmosphere of freedom and personal emancipation are likely to be shocked and disappointed. There are opportunities for creativity and self-expression, but they have to be made; the satisfactions of the job are subtle and complex, and come from balancing rival claims on time and energy, and over-coming obstacles and constraints. In many ways, social work embodies exaggerated versions of the dilemmas and problems of society at large, and is certainly not an escape from them. It does not, for instance, offer a haven from the fundamental tensions and conflicts between workers and management. Hence the increasing importance of trade unions in social work, which offer support and solidarity on many important issues, but add still further dilemmas – for example over the ethical justification of strikes which affect very vulnerable clients.

For all these reasons, while many social workers are happy, committed and fulfilled people who retain their freshness and enthusiasm after many years of hard work, others are jaded, careworn, depressed and listless. The phenomenon of 'burn-out' in social work has only recently received much attention. It consists in a recognizable tendency among workers under prolonged and intense stress to become unable to respond to their work in ways which match their original motivation or learnt skills. Instead they become defeated and defensive, and seem to avoid the difficult and demanding parts of the job, or respond to them in very negative ways. There are many theories about how this may occur, but all agree that it is due to stress. It seems unlikely that this is simple *quantitative* demand on the worker's energies. It is more likely to reflect a difficulty in reconciling competing or conflicting demands, perhaps simultaneously from clients, the agency and the worker's own family.

Several years ago I ran a one-day discussion group for experienced social workers, in which it quickly became apparent that several of the members were 'burnt-out'. They were cynical, critical, and made it clear that this participation was merely a ruse for getting away from the office for a day. I eventually got the group to look at crucial turning points in their lives, and especially their lives as social workers. The 'burnt-out' workers were able to identify quite clearly the moment at which the demands of the job became too much for them. Often they were working with enormous case-loads, covering for sick colleagues; the agency was putting extra stresses on them, and showing no appreciation (they felt) of their efforts; and the final straw was an illness or family problem at home. Their accounts were vivid and moving testimonies of the strains of social work, and the toll it can take on workers. Good intentions, even altruistic zeal, are not enough. A good social worker needs personal resilience, the support of colleagues and superiors, and a satisfying private life, to give of his best over a prolonged period.

THE CLIENT'S VIEW

So far I have described social work entirely from the point of view of the worker. What about the client's perspective? Research into the opinions of those on the receiving end of social work has only been undertaken fairly recently, and is still patchy. As might be expected the results are very mixed.

On the whole, elderly people are the most appreciative consumers of all the social services. They seem grateful for anything they receive – even from such notoriously unpopular agencies as supplementary benefits – and particularly value practical and material assistance, which enables them to continue to live in their own homes. From this point of view, the domiciliary services provided by local authority social services departments are particularly popular. It is ironical that services for the elderly, which are least likely to be performed by trained social workers, and which the majority of social workers themselves least enjoy providing, are those most appreciated by clients.

By contrast, trained field social workers *most* enjoy work with children and families. But this work includes preventive work (helping families stay intact) and work entails receiving children into care, or removing them compulsorily from their families. It is this last category of work which gives rise to most potential conflict. Nowadays a high proportion of children compulsorily removed from home are taken under Place of Safety Orders – a social worker comes to the house with a compulsory order, signed by a magistrate, and takes the children away with little or no notice, often against strong resistance from the parents. Also, the proportion of children in care whose parents lose their parental rights to the local authority (either through care orders by the courts, or through administrative transfer of these rights under the Children Act) has been rising. This in part reflects a policy by social workers of trying to arrange more permanent substitute care (including adoption) for children in care, which in turn involves excluding more parents from the lives of their children. (Many of these will already have lost contact with their children in care, but a few are being denied access, even if they have kept in touch.) All this has contributed to a good deal of hostility against social workers, particularly by parents who have experienced these conflicts, and by organizations representing, for instance, single parents. Researchers have encountered angry clients who described social workers as 'the Gestapo', and organizations like Gingerbread advise their members to be very wary of approaching social services departments.

For the rest, opinions are very varied. Here is a small sample of views from clients of a number of different agencies, statutory and voluntary:

Dissatisfied client, Family Welfare Association: The welfare lady came to the house one day when my husband was home and there was a big row between us. I got up to it with my husband and he got up to it with me. The welfare lady knew very well what I went through with my husband, but she just sat there and listened, and she never tried to do anything. She just listened and didn't drum any sense into my husband at all.[1]

Satisfied client, Family Welfare Assocition: The social worker was nice and pleasant and very polite and quiet in his ways. And sort of steady in asking the questions. The second time I went I felt a bit better in myself and the third time I felt even stronger. Each time I was able to tell him more of what happened. I felt as though he was giving me great strength, that I had someone behind me. I felt that if anything went really wrong, that I had him to go to.[2]

Juvenile delinquent: He doesn't do or say much – just soft questions –

can't understand him most of the time – is like a record player.[3]

Juvenile delinquent: He's all right – like him – he lets you discuss your family problems and your home. He's trying to get money to take us on a holiday but will be all canoeing and that.[4]

Family casework client: I don't know what her job should be, but she's not much help.[5]

Family casework client: She does a lot more than her job. When her time is up, she goes a bit beyond to try to help me, whereas other social workers would just go home.[6]

Social services client: I think if your face fits you're in; I think you've got to give them a hard luck story, cry and go right down as if you are one bag of nerves.[7]

Social services client: I think that before they see to the immigrants they should see to the English people.[8]

Child in care: My brother and I have had more social workers that I can remember. They'd see us once and then disappear for six months, then we'd have a new one. And it's been going on all the time I've been in the home. They've been leaving or they've been going ill. And if that's happening all the time, I don't see how they can help you.[9]

A few weeks ago children from a teenage hostel threatened with closure personally lobbied councillors from the floor of Solihull Council Chamber and succeeded in overturning its previous decision to close the home.[10]

WIDER VIEWS OF SOCIAL WORK

In recent years, British social workers have been heavily criticized by the press, and seem to be held in low public esteem. However, such research as has been done reveals that the bad press which social work has received on some (mainly child care) issues does not reflect overall opinion. Most people think that someone should do most of the things that social workers do. But there is profound disagreement about how they should do them, whether they should be paid for doing them, and if so, whether they should be employed by the state. In this book, I shall try to disentangle some of the origins of these disputes, and look at how British social work has come to take its current shape. Above all, since most of the fiercest disputes are about the role of local authority social workers, I shall consider some of the contradictions of that role.

Many of the disputes at the heart of these matters concern the nature and origins of the social problems and needs that social workers tackle. These problems are near enough to our day-to-day experiences to allow us to have strong opinions on them. In this sense they are small-scale, personal problems of everyday life – commonsense matters, that call forth domestic or parochial resources for their solutions. But in another sense they raise profound political and ideological issues about the nature of society itself, and the role of the state.

For instance, there is general agreement that old people should not be allowed to starve in filth and squalor, but very little about how to prevent this happening, or who should be held responsible if it does. Is it evidence of inadequate state provision, the isolation of modern urban life, or neglectful neighbours and kin?

The ways in which public services mesh in with informal neighbourhood and family networks are far more subtle and complex than is commonly imagined. There are enormous gaps in public consciousness of social problems – 'no go' areas, where we as private citizens prefer to turn a blind eye, rather than endure the discomfort of having to do something about persistent suffering or injustice. It is only when these spill out, in highly visible forms, that public and political demands for action by the social services are heard.

Child abuse is one clear example of this. There is no real evidence that more children are hurt, neglected or killed nowadays than in any previous era – if anything, statistics suggest that in recent years social services departments have become more effective at the basic task of protecting vulnerable infants. What is clear is that neither before child abuse became a national issue, nor since, have neighbours and kin (who must always have been aware of the problem) been willing to tackle it directly. Before Maria Colwell, hundreds of children must have died in circumstances which raised profound suspicions in their neighbours and extended families, but where such suspicions were suppressed, or somehow 'managed' within these networks. What has changed is not the inability of these networks to prevent such tragedies; it is public awareness that there exists an agency – social services departments – onto which all the guilt, anxiety and responsibility for such a situation can be off-loaded.

The vast majority of social problems and needs that the public is willing to recognize as such are met by informal neighbourhood resources. But there remain an enormous number of latent problems, half-recognized or ignored, which constitute potential time-bombs in any community. It is these that, once they explode into public consciousness, become the stuff of controversy about the role of local authority social workers.

It is in these situations that cries go up for rapid and decisive action by social workers, and in its absence the strongest criticisms are made. Public consciousness sees no contradiction in allowing lay opinions much weight in such matters, yet expecting social workers to show professional skill and judgement in affairs which laymen (and especially neighbours) carefully avoid.

The boundary areas between the family and neighbourhood on the one hand, and social work (and particularly local authority social services departments) on the other, are areas of confusion and dispute. What is at issue is the nature and extent of personal responsibility and responsibility for others in a shared network. In modern British society there are no absolute standards in these matters. Our society contains innumerable anomalies, anachronisms and contradictions. There are small rural hamlets where social relations have been little affected by the industrial revolution, and inner-city ghettos populated mainly by post-war immigrants. In these very diverse communities, boundaries are drawn at quite different points.

Every referral of an individual or family to a social work agency entails negotiations about these boundaries; a referral to the local social services department entails negotiations with an official representative of the state.

The state has certain expectations of how families should behave towards their dependants, and the circumstances in which their efforts should be supplemented or superseded. These expectations contain elements of flexibility and adaptability to local circumstances, even though many of them are laid down by statute (e.g. child care, mental health and public hygiene legislation). However, they also depend on local resources, and the ideological complexion of the political party in power.

In many rural or suburban communities, incursions by social workers are rare, and mainly concern problems which have been festering for years, but which finally break out of the framework of local neighbourhood management. Yet there are also inner-city areas where it is normal for social workers to be involved with most households; where they come and go without the courtesy of letters or appointments; where their visits are as expected a part of life as those of kin and neighbours; where people consult social workers about day-to-day aspects of their family relationships and their dealings with other arms of officialdom. Such high concentrations of social work tend to correlate with at least one other indicator of a 'social problem area' – high rates of male unemployment, large proportions of single parent families or high rates of juvenile delinquency. In such areas, social work is not a 'last resort', where neighbourhood methods of problem management break down. It is rather part of the apparatus by which the state monitors and controls a proportion of the population – the inner-city poor – whose social role has itself become problematic.

With economic stagnation and mass unemployment, a substantial and growing number of people have no obvious contribution to make to the productive process. Such people often live in subsidized and rent-rebated local authority housing, on state benefits, or work in state-assisted job creation schemes. To call them the 'industrial reserve army', (to use Marx's term) is perhaps over-optimistic, since it is unlikely that British industry will require their services again in an age of automation. They might be more accurately described, in the nineteenth-century term, as 'surplus population'. Although they receive disproportionate attention from most official agencies, including the police, it is social workers who give the closest attention to the quality of their personal lives.

This is itself involves as many difficult boundaries as work in more settled and prosperous communities. Social work in such 'problem' neighbourhoods is by no means politically and morally neutral. The state is concerned to define the limits of its help to such people – to ration its resources in such a way as to reinforce personal and family responsibilities. Social work supplements this fixed ration of assistance, and reinforces the need for limits, by imposing rationing of its own, more detailed and personal kind. Similarly, the state is concerned to control the potential threat posed by this section of the population, which has so little obvious stake in the existing social order. Social workers exercise control over such sensitive areas as child care and delinquency, with the power to remove children and adolescents from the most deviant families, and to enforce standards on the rest. Seen in this light, the role of social workers in certain neighbourhoods – and at the time of writing the male unemployment rate amongst blacks in Brixton was 70 per cent, and amongst all males on some Glasgow estates over 60 per cent – is the time-honoured one of public assistance agencies; regulating the poor.

Yet most social workers would want to disclaim this restrictive definition of their tasks. They would see social work as inseparably connected with helping, and with doing so in a distinctively personal and caring way. Thus there is an inevitable tension between the expectations of many politicians and much of the ratepaying public, and the aspirations of social workers themselves, with their clients' needs and wishes forming the third side of a problematic triangle.

THE DAILY DRAMA

This scenario for state social work with a largely unmotivated or actively resistant clientele has enormous potential for tragi-comedy. The social worker is trapped between competing demands, and has often to acknowledge the absurdity of his situation. He may well need a sense of humour to survive. Here are two examples. The first is from an account by a group of residential child care workers of an experimental project in an inner city which attempted to keep (mainly black) teenagers in care within their local community. The project workers struggled not only with the disruptive behaviour of their resident adolescents, but also with the problems of their relationships with 'outsiders', both friendly and hostile. Here is a sample of the workers' diary (the names are of residents unless otherwise stated):

Sunday, 24 November, 1974 . . . approx. 5.00 a.m. front door bell rang. Mandy dumped by a taxi, very drunk or stoned. Collapsed on floor. Paul and I tried to carry her to bed. After about 15 minutes she became more conscious and started screaming, shouting for Icah, her boyfriend who had dumped her out of the taxi as he thought she was going out with the 'Ladbroke Grove' boys. Wanted to go looking for him, claiming he was going to break into a shop and she was going to stop him. Wouldn't let her go. . . .

Tuesday, 3 December, 1974 . . . approx. 10.00 p.m. the 'black mini' with the Ladbroke Grove boys inside pulled up outside. They knocked the door and wanted to come in. Washington said 'no' and a quarrel started. Kipper (staff) happened to be there and said to them that if Washington didn't want them they should go. A bit of a fight broke out between Washington and the black mini boys and Kipper shut the door. One of the black mini boys slung an axe through the frong door, narrowly missing Kipper. Resisted phoning the police immediately. Went down to Washington's bedsit where there were approx. 13 kids, most of whom we recognized as Mandy's friends. Asked them all to leave which they did quickly. The black mini had left a long time ago. Police arrived. Called by a neighbour presumably. We told them briefly what happened but said we didn't want to report it at this point. They left. We then talked with Mandy, Washington and Paul about pros and cons of telling police officially. After a lot of discussion we decided to tell police officially as feeling was that if we didn't they'd just come back and the same thing would happen. Talked about the implications of this to project and residents generally, particularly Mandy. . . . Phoned police and PC Washbourne came down. Quite helpful. . . . Decided to say to police we wouldn't charge, but that police should hold a general description of mini until 10.00 p.m. tomorrow night when we'll contact them and tell them if we want to proceed or not. . . .

Wednesday, 4 December, 1974 . . . Lads from Grove turned up at 8.15 p.m., quite willing to talk about incident – expressed regret and will pay for damage to door. Will bring money round on Saturday morning. Felt it necessary to show goodwill and develop trust. . . . [11]

The second example is from my own experience. In my book *Helping in Social Work*, I gave an account of the following absurd experience, concerning an ageing ex-seaman, ex-prisoner and ex-tramp, Mr Peterson, whom I had helped to settle down nearby:

He used sometimes to come into town to get drunk, and ring up more for the lift home than anything else. One market day he rang when I was home for tea. I said I would meet him in the bus station a few minutes later. I found him leaning against a wall in a busy concourse, bemoaning his fate. 'I can't go on, Bill, I can't take any more. I'm better off inside. At least the Governor always gives me a decent job.' He rocked precariously to and fro in his nautical garb, like a bosun in a high wind. At this point Jackie, a young woman who was also under my supervision, walked by with her three-year-old daughter. The little girl detached herself from her mother and started to swing on my leg, shrieking in a high-pitched voice, 'Sweeties, Jordan, I want some sweeties.' I suggested to the swaying mariner that we should go into the bus station cafe for a cup of tea, and we staggered off with the little girl still in tow. The cafe was very full, and we jostled a few elbows and sloshed a few cups as we lurched towards the counter. While Mr Peterson was ordering his refreshment, the little girl kept wailing that she couldn't see the sweeties, so I hoisted her up to give her a better view. Suddenly she was snatched from my grasp by a furious mother (who must have lost track of her in the crowds) indignantly shouting, 'What the hell are you doing with my child?' Fifty heads swivelled and shocked looks bored into me. Drunken sailor and blushing child molester found themselves seats as quickly as possible.[12]

These examples illustrate, in a rather extreme form, the day-to-day stresses that make social work a demanding and exhausting occupation. They also show how it is of the essence of social work that national social problems – unemployment, race relations, delinquency, single parent-hood – should find their distillation in a series of personal and moral dilemmas confronting the social worker. The pain, confusion, distress, bitterness and rebellion of his clients, as they struggle against such adverse circumstances, present him with perplexing and potentially paralysing choices between action and inaction.

The aim of this book is not to 'resolve' all these dilemmas and confusions, but to illustrate some of their origins and consequences. The invitation to social work is not to a tranquil haven of serene altruism, but to a fragmented hotch-potch which reflects the hypocrisies, the heroisms and the heartlessnesses of wider society.

It also aims to clarify why people become social workers, and how social work fits into the welfare state and wider British society. To do this, it is organized into three main sections, each reflecting important traditions which form part of social work. The first is concerned with the personal processes of helping those in distress; the second with the social services in a modern industrial state; and the third with the critical and political aspects of social work and social policy. In the final part I shall give examples of how these dilemmas may be tackled in practice.

REFERENCES

1 J. E. Mayer and N. Timms, *The Client Speaks: Working Class Impression of Casework*, Routledge & Kegan Paul, 1970, p. 69

2 *Ibid.*, p. 84

3 Howard Parker, Maggie Casburn and David Turnbull, *Receiving Juvenile Justice: Adolescents and State Care and Control*, Basil Blackwell, 1981, p. 125

4 *Ibid.*, p. 124

5 Eric Sainsbury, Stephen Nixon and David Phillips, *Social Work in Focus: Clients' and Social Workers' Perceptions in Long-Term Social Work*, Routledge & Kegan Paul, 1982, p. 78

6 *Ibid.*, p. 78

7 Carole Satyamurti, *Occupational Survival: The Case of the Local Authority Social Worker*, Basil Blackwell, 1981, p. 114

8 *Ibid.*, p. 115

9 National Children's Bureau, *'Who Cares?' Young People in Care Speak Out*, NCB Conference, 1975, p. 35

10 *Social Work Today*

11 Fatma Dharamsi, *et al.*, *Caring for Children: A Diary of a Local Authority Children's Home*, Owen Wells, 1979, pp. 29, 37

12 Bill Jordan, *Helping in Social Work*, Routledge & Kegan Paul, 1979, pp. 119–20

PART I
The Perfect Friend

2

Good Advice

In simple societies there are no social workers. Orphans, widows, handicapped people and the elderly are looked after within the extended family or the tribe. Unconventional behaviour is either tolerated, venerated or punished by retributive methods. The notion of having specialists in planning the care of dependants, or in changing the non-conforming behaviour of other people, is largely a creation of modern industrial societies.

Many historical strands contributed to the role of the modern social worker. They included the church traditions from the Middle Ages; the earliest state services, provided at a parish level under the Poor Laws; the development of the 'ancient professions' of law, medicine and education; and the charitable societies of the nineteenth century.

Each of these traditions gave something to social work's identity, through its organization or its working methods. The most obvious organizational antecedents of social work lie in the Poor Law tradition, which emerged with embryonic state social services in all the European countries and in Britain with the formation of modern nation states. As part of their more total responsibility for the ordering of society, and with the break-up of the feudal economic and social structures, central governments set up local institutions and networks of services for the management of poverty, vagrancy and petty crime.

It is difficult to reconstruct the quality of these early services. Our perceptions of the Poor Law are heavily

31

overlaid by accounts of its operation in the nineteenth century, when a deliberately harsh and punitive purpose was introduced into its administration. Earlier parish records tend to be brief, and more concerned to record sums disbursed, or itinerants dispersed, than the quality of the human relations behind such decisions.

It is therefore usual to trace the origins of social work to a third tradition, which did not fully emerge until the nineteenth century, and which had as its key the development of a leisured class. Particularly significant was the emergence of the educated middle-class woman. It is important to emphasize that this tradition contributed only one element, but a very important one – the notion of the importance of *personal relationships* to the process of social rehabilitation. In this chapter I shall concentrate on this strand of social work, which is still one of its essential features.

The nineteenth century was the heyday of voluntary charitable societies of all sorts – religious and missionary bodies, highly specialized societies and groups interested in an enormous range of social phenomena. Working-class folk memories of charitable ladies convey them as moralistic busybodies in ridiculous hats, and so undoubtedly many of them were. But others were unquestionably committed and dedicated to an extraordinary degree, combining formidable energy with a sensitive compassion for people in the extremes of distress.

In many fields, the best of these charitable ladies offered 'perfect friendship' to the most socially and morally degraded members of society. Elizabeth Fry with prisoners, Josephine Butler with prostitutes, Octavia Hill with slum tenants, made enormous sacrifices of time and emotional energy, giving these people a mixture of Christian love and practical advice. In a rather more organizing way, Florence Nightingale and Mary Carpenter offered something of the same to the sick, and juvenile delinquents. Against the harsh background of Britain in the process of industrialization and urbanization, and increasingly divided on class lines, they represented a model of a *personal* relationship between the fortunate and favoured classes and the most demoralized victims of social change.

Victorian charity played an important role in the social policy of that era. Industrialization had been accompanied by a political commitment to individual rights and liberties, and to the maximization of economic freedoms. This led to an insistence that the poor – including the enormous new urban proletariat who had been drawn in by rising industrial wages – must take their chance in the free market, unprotected by the state. The new Poor Law of 1834 was largely a system for excluding the able-bodied from relief, defining eligibility in terms requiring personal degradation and loss of citizenship. But side by side with this official harshness went fear of a whole new class which threatened social cohesion, internal security and pubic morals. Hence the twin themes of social *investigation* – anxious research into the numbers and habits of the urban poor – and charity. The task of classifying the poor, and giving 'scientific assistance' according to moral status, complemented the narrow exclusiveness of the poor law, and provided a network of inclusion and distribution through voluntary agencies, which subtly reinforced the moral regime of the middle classes. This British development of the second half of the nineteenth century was echoed – at a similar stage of economic development – in the early twentieth century in the USA.

Charity was also of ideological importance. It enabled the new middle classes to justify their privileges, and to insist that capital accumulation and private property need not lead to an increasing gulf between rich and poor. The examples of the best of the early social workers – even though they were a tiny, unrepresentative group – were held up as emblems of class altruism and compassion. They also allowed a new kind of middle-class identity and sensibility, embodying many of the ideals which had been taking shape in emerging bourgeois consciousness, and influencing every later generation of young idealists, motivated by 'social conscience'.

What were the characteristics of these 'perfect friendships' which were the forerunners of all our subsequent social work attempts at the 'helping relationship'? They were humble, never patronizing; they emphasized common humanity and the universality of sin; they held out the hope of God's forgiveness and of spiritual regeneration, but also of practical steps towards material and physical rehabilitation; they were generous in their offers of time and attention; they conveyed God's acceptance through their own empathy and kindness. As a result, these earliest social workers were often perceived by their clients as both exceptionally human and exceptionally saintly.

The work of these middle-class Victorian heroines, amply documented in their own time, was paralleled – and in some cases prefigured – by fictional accounts of similar paragons of good works. Indeed, the history of the novel closely documents the history of such relationships. By a remarkable coincidence, Daniel Defoe, author of what is widely regarded as the first novel of the modern era, gives us a glimpse of the quality of such 'perfect friendship' in his account of the prison chaplain in *The Fortunes and Misfortunes of Moll Flanders*, published in 1722. It is far from clear how representative of early eighteenth-century chaplains this man was; but it does indicate how closely the Victorian model of social work was based on a puritan tradition of religious counselling. The example is so striking that it seems worth quoting at some length. Moll Flanders, twice married and twice ruined, has been arrested for her part in the activities of a professional gang of thieves, sent to Newgate prison, and sentenced to death by hanging. At the point when her senses have been dulled by despair, and only days before her execution, the chaplain approaches her:

The minister pressed me to tell him, as far as I thought convenient, in what state I found myself as to the sight I had of things beyond life. He told me that he did not come as an ordinary of the place, whose business it is to extort confessions from prisoners, for private ends, or for the further detecting of other offenders; that his business was to move me to such freedom of discourse as might serve to disburthen my own mind, and furnish him to administer comfort to me as far as was in his power; and assured me that whatever I said to him should remain with him, and be as much a secret as if it was known only to God and myself; and that he desired to know nothing of me, but as above, to qualify him to apply proper advice and assistance to me, and to pray to God for me.

This honest, friendly way of treating me unlocked all the sluices of my passions. He broke into my very soul by it; and I unravelled all the wickedness of my life to him. . . .

I hid nothing from him, and he in return exhorted me to sincere repentance, explained to me what he meant by repentance, and then drew out such a scheme of infinite mercy, proclaimed from heaven to sinners of the greatest magnitude, that he left me nothing to say, that looked like despair, or doubting of being accepted. . . .

I am not able to repeat the excellent discourses of this extraordinary man; 'tis all that I am able to do, to say that he revived my heart, and brought me into such a condition that I never knew anything of in my life before. I was covered with shame and tears for things past, and yet at the same time a secret surprising joy at the prospect of being a true penitent. . . .[1]

This vivid account of emotional catharsis suggests that Elizabeth Fry – a devout Quaker – had a clear model for her work in the ministrations of much earlier puritan parsons. Like Elizabeth Fry herself, some hundred years later, the fictional prison chaplain was as concerned to get reprieves as he was to achieve repentances, and in Moll's case he was successful in both respects. Later still, George Eliot provided a much more developed account of the same process in *Adam Bede*, where Dinah Morris, an itinerant Methodist preacher, unlocks the heart of her unfortunate cousin Hetty Sorrell, awaiting execution for infanticide, before she is reprieved through the intervention of her seducer.

In Dickens' novels, this new style of charitable compassion is depicted alongside the self-righteous, moralistic, overbearing, disrespectful or distant forms which it sought to displace. In *Bleak House*, the heroine, Esther Summerson, is modest and self-effacing, perceptive of others' needs, aware but in control of her own. She has a keen moral sense, but is also tolerant and non-judgemental. Above all, she is capable of great self-sacrifice, as when she ministers to the dying crossing-sweeper Jo, and thus contracts an illness which causes her permanent disfigurement.

By contrast, Dickens presents us with an assortment of people whose charitable works serve mainly to impress others or delude themselves. In particular, there is Mrs Jellyby, who 'could see nothing nearer than Africa'[2] and neglects her own household in pursuing (by correspondence) the welfare of the natives of Borrioboola-Gha, on the left bank of the Niger; and Mrs Pardiggle, the tireless visitor of the poor. Accompanying the latter to the house of some impoverished brickmakers, where she had left some religious tracts for their edifiction, Esther observes Mrs Pardiggle's 'mechanical way of taking possession of people'[3] and her tendency to take them into religious custody 'as if she were an inexorable moral Policeman carrying them all off to a station-house.'[4] She also hears one of the brickmakers give Mrs Pardiggle a classic client's reply to uninvited welfare intrusion:

'I wants it done, and over. I wants a end of these liberties took with my place. I wants a end of being drawed like a badger. Now you're a-going to polly-pry and question according to custom – I know what you're a-going to be up to. Well! You haven't got no occasion to be up to it. I'll save you the trouble. Is my daughter a-washin? Yes she *is* a-washin. Look at the water. Smell it! That's wot we drinks. How do you like it, and what do you think of gin instead! Ain't my place dirty? Yes it is dirty – it's nat'rally dirty, and it's nat'rally onwholesome; and we've had five dirty and onwholesome children, as is all dead infants, and so much the better for them, and for us besides. Have I read the little book wot you left? No, I ain't read the little book wot you left. There ain't nobody here as knows how to read it; and if there wos, it wouldn't be suitable to me. It's a book fit for a babby, and I'm not a babby. . . . How have I been conducting myself? Why, I've been drunk for three days; and I'd a been drunk for four, if I'd had the money. . . . And how did my wife get that black eye? Why, I giv' it her, and if she says I didn't, she's a Lie!'[5]

Through Esther and her eventual husband, Dr Alan Woodcourt, Dickens indicates the qualities and experience that he regards as essential for breaking down 'the iron barrier'[6] between Mrs Pardiggle and the brickmakers. These should be developed initially through the personal and family relationships of the would-be helper. Early in the book, Esther lists the qualifications she lacks for the charitable work that Mrs Pardiggle had invited her to undertake:

That I was inexperienced in the art of adapting my mind to minds very differently situated, and addressing them from suitable points of view. That I had not that delicate knowledge of the heart that must be essential to such a work. That I had much to learn, myself, before I could teach others, and that I could not confide in my good intentions alone. For these reasons, I thought it best to be as useful as I could, and to render what kind services I could, to those immediately about me; and to try to let that circle of duty gradually and naturally expand itself.[7]

It is clear from literary passages such as this one, and from the writings of the leading social workers themselves, that these Victorians made little distinciton between the ideals of friendship and the values that informed their charity. Octavia Hill, who pioneered methods of housing management based on these principles, insisted that what the poor needed was 'not alms but a friend'. 'By friendship she meant giving all her resources to the common pool of daily life in which she shared as an equal.'[8] The defining quality of her relationships with her tenants and the pupils in her schools was 'respectfulness', an acknowledgement of their human dignity and of the moral significance of every aspect of the relationship between them. These values are still fundamental to the ethical code claimed by modern social workers.

There was a remarkable consistency in the application of many of these early social workers of their moral principles to their lives; yet to modern eyes there were also many contradictions. Elizabeth Fry began visiting prisons in 1813. She befriended the most despairing and degraded female prisoners in the squalor of Newgate and started a school for prisoners' children there. After encountering opposition from the prison authorities, she and her fellow members of the Association for the Improvement of the Female Prisoners in Newgate persuaded the governor to let them run sewing classes which (with the full co-operation of the prisoners) transformed the moral climate of the prison. Her system of work and religious instruction was spread to other prisons and ships used for transportation. But at the same time as revolutionizing prison discipline, she was in day-to-day communication with Lord Sidmouth, the devious and spiteful

Home Secretary in one of the most repressive governments Britain has suffered, and thus – modern radicals would argue – oiling the wheels of political oppression while pleading for the lives of women sentenced to hang. She also became an international figure, advising the King of Prussia (that sworn foe of Liberalism) on prison reform.

Octavia Hill was brought up by her grandfather, Dr Southwood Smith, the sanitary reformer. As a young woman she was involved with the Christian Socialist movement, became a friend of Ruskin's, and started a school in a slum area of London in the 1850s. With money she borrowed from Ruskin, she bought a delapidated row of workmen's cottages, and set about the physical improvement of the buildings and the moral regeneration of her tenants. In spite of intimidation and threats, she insisted both on personal contacts with all of them, and on regular payments of rent. She created a communal room for a social centre and crèche, and a playground for children, involving the tenants themselves in every stage of their organization. In addition to transforming the physical and social environment, she made a profit, paying Ruskin back in 18 months. Her energy (despite poor health) and detailed attention were enormous. She treated tenants as 'friends and equals'. Yet she was equally energetic in pursuit of fraud and false pretences amongst claimants of charitable aid. Just as her housing management principles spread through London, so did her strict precepts for charity. By 1885 she owned 130 houses in Deptford alone; but she was campaigning against state housing, state pensions and even the Salvation Army, because they did not conform to her principles of personal investigation. She served on the Royal Commission investigating the Reform of the Poor Laws from 1905 and 1909, and died in 1912, a firm opponent of women's suffrage.

MORAL EDUCATION

It was a strength rather than a weakness of these pioneers that they saw their work primarily in moral terms. As Dickens illustrated in *Bleak House*, moral education could be achieved through simplicity, humility, courage and commitment, and need not imply the patronizing, superior attitude of the Pardiggles. Indeed, the great novelists all indicate that Victorian notions of friendship encompassed this ideal. As the critic Lionel Trilling suggests, they illustrate a principle of 'intelligent love', that 'the finest and deepest relationship that can exist between human beings is pedagogic' and 'consists in giving and receiving knowledge about right conduct, in the formation of one person's character by another, the acceptance of another's guidance in one's growth.'[9]

Perhaps the earliest literary expression of this ideal was Jane Austen's *Mansfield Park*. The heroine, Fanny Price, is a quiet, retiring girl, brought up in the household of her rich, vivid and sophisticated relatives, the Bertrams. That she retains her strong sense of identity and earnest moral purpose is largely owing to her relationship with her cousin Edmund, who is destined for the ministry. Towards the end of the book, Fanny visits her parents' home in Portsmouth after a long absence, and is shocked by the laxity of its standards. She shares a room with her sullen and rebellious younger sister, Susan, and gradually their relationship develops, as Susan confides in Fanny:

Her temper was open. She acknowledgd her fears, blamed herself for having contended so warmly, and from that hour Fanny, understanding the worth of her disposition, and perceiving how fully she was inclined to seek her good opinion and refer to her judgement, began to feel again the blessing of affection, and to entertain the hope of being useful to a mind so much in need of help, and so much deserving it. She gave advice; advice too sound to be resisted by a good understanding, and given too mildly and considerately as not to irritate an imperfect temper; and she had the happiness of observing its good effects not infrequently; more was not expected by one, who, while seeing all the obligation and expediency of submission and forbearance, saw also with sympathetic acuteness of feeling, all that must be hourly grating to a girl like Susan. Her greatest wonder on the subject soon became – not that Susan should have been provoked into disrespect and against her better knowledge – but that so much better knowledge, so many good notions, should have been hers at all; and that, brought up in the midst of negligence and error, she should have formed such proper opinions of what ought to be – she, who had no cousin Edmund to direct her thoughts or fix her principles.[10]

It would be wrong to suggest that the early social workers were always so compassionate and so humble as their precepts seem to imply. Certain roles – especially those connected with poor relief – evinced reactions from them which would strike most modern social workers as harsh and judgemental. The Charity Organization Society (of which Octavia Hill was a leading light) sought to introduce scientific principles of almsgiving, based on thorough investigation of the habits and modes of life of applicants. Only about one in three were actually assisted under its regime – those who were judged to have been 'reduced to distress without fault or improvidence of their own, even persons who had not made the best use of their opportunities, but whose previous position and temperament would make the workhouse almost intolerable'.[11] For the rest, the charitable organizers left a choice between fending for themselves, or subjection to a Poor Law system which they recommended should be made 'as distasteful as possible to the applicants'.[12] The Society's objectives included 'the promotion of habits of providence and self-reliance, and of those social and sanitary principles, the observance of which is essential to the well-being of the poor and of the community at large', and 'the repression of mendicity and imposture'.[13]

It never seemed to occur to these middle-class people, who could sacrifice so many of their educational and material advantages, and often their health itself, to the cause of 'perfect friendship' with the poor, that collective state provision to alleviate poverty and improve the environment might achieve more than the personal example they offered. When state provision became a political issue, the great majority of early social workers were implacably opposed to collective action.

The key to this apparently paradoxical combination of compassion and harshness seems to lie in the notion of society as an organism, and of individuals within it as partaking in a common moral life. According to the favourite philosophers of the Victorian bourgeoisie – John Stuart Mill and T. H. Green in particular – the organic wholeness of society overrode economic differences and conflicts of interest. Just as the economic choices of each individual in the free market, and the competition between rival enterprises, contributed to the maximum material output of society, and to the expansion of wealth, so the moral choices of individuals and the cooperation of freely-chosen associates led to the health and growth of the moral organism of society. Compulsory collective action – in the economic or the social sphere – necessarily distorted or stunted this process, coming between individuals and their developing relationships. Both inequalities of wealth and ruin for the unfortunate were part of the price to be paid for the essential freedoms on which this system was based.

Hence the Victorians were, in a sense, far more radical in their application of the principle of individual 'self-determination' than modern social workers, even though the latter still claim it as part of their ethical code. John Stuart Mill – himself a sensitive and sympathetic person – robustly asserted:

that the sole end for which mankind are warranted, individually or collectively, in interfering with the liberty of action of any of their number, is self-protection. The only purpose for which power can rightfully be exercised over any member of a civilized society, against his will, is to prevent harm to others. His own good, either physical or moral, is not a sufficient warrant.[14]

Similarly, Octavia Hill argued that 'Each man has had his own view of life and must be free to fulfil it. . . . In many ways he is a far better judge of it than we, as he has lived through himself what we have only seen.'[15]

For these Victorians, there was no distinction between social and moral duties. Both were derived from anxioms of conduct – essentially Christian – which were outside and beyond the individual himself. Personal fulfilment and social obligation were not rival claims on the individual; both could be pursued simultaneously through the same moral rules.

This allowed the early social workers to make categorical and absolute judgements on standards of behaviour, without moral or social relativity. It also meant that poverty and homelessness could usually be seen as personal failures rather than as products of the economic system. But because the individual and society were seen as potentially in harmony, social workers were also confident in the social significance of their work. Far from being narrowly concerned with individuals and families, someone like Octavia Hill moved easily and naturally between casework, group work, residential provision and community work, taking an interest in tenants' associations, recreational and neighbourhood facilities, and the conservation of the countryside, and seeing no tensions or contradictions between these aspects of her work.

There was an active, organizing aspect of Victorian social work that went well beyond the mere 'counselling' of people in distress. They would have considered our modern distinctions between 'methods' of social work, and our divisions of labour, entirely artificial or actually misleading. The only meaningful division for them was between voluntary organizations, in which they saw the potential for benevolent action, and the state, whose services should be minimal. Right up to the First World War, social work presupposed both class privilege and the sacrifice of class advantages in the service of less fortunate souls. For instance, Clement Attlee came to socialism through social work when, as a young ex-public schoolboy he became involved in a boys' club in the East End of London.

DISSOLUTION OF THE MORAL CONSENSUS

The onset of doubts about the moral basis of social work can be traced to the first quarter of this century, both in Britain and the USA. The doubts concerned the personal and political integrity of the privileged 'helper'; they stemmed ultimately (though often remotely) from the insights of Freud and Marx. Freud showed that the human heart was not an open book, and that people could not (even with goodwill and good faith) give an accurate account of the motives, still less the moral principles, which determined their actions. They were, in fact, driven by dark and irrational forces within them, which remained unconscious, and the clues to which only emerged in dreams and slips of the tongue. These instinctual drives, with their basis in sexuality, were universal, and hence as much a part of the helper's psyche as that of the client. Worst of all, the irrational forces of the unconscious could reach out to each other across the divide between persons, leaving their most well-meaning 'owners' almost as helpless spectators. Thus Freud described the phenomena of 'transference' (women patients falling in love with their male psychoanalysts, for instance) and countertransference (the therapist's emotional response). Hints of the same insights into the powerful and uncontrollably irrational drives governing the closest of relationships were also to be found in the novels of Thomas Hardy and D. H. Lawrence.

Marx's work attacked the 'social organism' model of society and the notion of harmonious economic progress. He revealed the hidden exploitation in capitalist relations of production, and showed how it required entrepreneurs to extract more and more unpaid labour from workers, to allow the accumulation of privately-owned means of production. The capitalist bourgeoisie and the industrial proletariat were thus classes with irreconcilable interests, and economic development could only produce a society in which these conflicts became more and more apparent. Marx's ideas, even if they did not predominate in working-class organizations in Britain, seemed to describe the general development of politics at the end of the nineteenth century, especially in Germany and France. The proletariat was becoming more conscious of itself, more organized, and less willing to accept middle-class definitions of its needs and interests. It wanted a say in its own future, and was willing to fight to get it. Novelists like Emile Zola in France, and George Gissing and Robert Tresall in Britain, documented the emergence of this new working class consciousness and struggle.

Both the psychological profundities of Freud and the political polemics of the socialists attacked the moral basis of

Victorian social work. The 'excellent discourses' of the pioneers were no longer enough. Some other underpinnings had to be sought. The disintegration of the old ethic and attempts at new syntheses will be examined in the next chapter.

REFERENCES

1 Daniel Defoe, *The Fortunes and Misfortunes of Moll Flanders* (1722), Penguin
2 Charles Dickens, *Bleak House*, Vol. 1 (1852), Chapman & Hall, 1911, p. 44
3 *Ibid.*, p. 131
4 *Ibid.*
5 *Ibid.*, pp. 130–1
6 *Ibid.*, p. 31
7 *Ibid.*, p. 127
8 Una Cormack, 'Developments in Casework', in *Voluntary Social Services*, ed. A. Bourdillon, Methuen, 1945, p. 97
9 Lionel Trilling, *Sincerity and Authenticity*, Oxford University Press, 1972, p. 82
10 Jane Austen, *Mansfield Park*, (1814), Williams & Norgate, 1948, pp. 328–9
11 Charity Organization Society, Second Annual Report, 1870, pp. 5–6
12 *Ibid.*
13 Charity Organization Society, Fifth Annual Report, 1875, pp. 5–6
14 J. S. Mill, *Essay on Liberty* (1859), Blackwell, 1946, p. 9
15 Una Cormack, *Oxford and Early Social Work*, unpublished

3

Wise Counselling

At the beginning of the twentieth century, and particularly
during and after the First World War, social work faced a
crisis in its identity, arising from psychological and political
challenges to its basic assumptions. If improvidence and anti-
social behaviour were not the results merely of ignorance, but
of deeper psychological processes – to which even the middle
classes were subject – then moral instruction, however
sincere, was inadequate or misplaced. If class interests could
not be harmonized through economic progress, if development actually sharpened class conflicts, then voluntary
benevolence was no answer to poverty and squalor.

These doubts were doubly powerful because they struck
simultaneously at the personal basis of the social worker's
commitment, and at the political foundations of the new
profession. They therefore gnawed away at the very roots
of social work, at a time when the state was cautiously
expanding its scope of intervention in the fields of income
maintenance, housing and health. The promise of collective
provision for decent minimum standards of living for all
citizens sustained the organized working class, and its new
political organ, the Labour Party, throughout the period of
high unemployment and widespread poverty between the
wars. Many idealistic young people, who had been social
workers before the First World War – like Attlee and Dalton –
became politicians in the Labour cause.

Before the First World War, the leading social workers had
been people held in high public esteem, who were consulted

about important social policy decisions. They sat on the Royal Commission on the Poor Laws, and subscribed to the Majority Report on how this major instrument for dealing with poverty should be modernized and adapted. Social work seemed to be about to become one of the major new professions in a changing world, and one which would attract many brilliant and idealistic people. After the First World War, no such prospects opened up. Instead, the dominant perceptions of political developments, class relations and even personal problems altered, leaving social workers stranded and trapped in old modes of thinking, acting and being.

But the world did not change quickly or dramatically, in spite of the shift in the moral climate. Instead it remained stubbornly stuck and stagnant, in an uncomfortable hiatus, when old values had become outmoded, yet new ones had not properly emerged. Social work became identified with old, stale, and increasingly discredited approaches to human problems – at least in its voluntary and charitable guises. It must have been a very painful period for its practitioners in those agencies, in which many of them undoubtedly became aware of the inadequacy of their ideas and methods, yet not many could devise new ways in response to new situations.

In trying to find a fictional account which gives a flavour of what this era must have been like, I turned to Paul Scott's novels about the last years of the British Raj. Although the parallels between the moral collapse of British rule in India and the decay in the values which underpinned social work may not seem obvious, I believe that they are enlightening. Scott's novels illustrate the dilemmas of all forms of benevolence based on privilege and class distinction when they come face-to-face with the beginnings of a demand for personal and political equality from the subject class or race. In particular, they suggest that the decay of a moral order is experienced in deeply personal as well as political terms, and most painfully by individuals who are attempting to reach across the gulf created by class and racial conflict. In this sense they are also relevant for today's social workers in South Africa, and possibly in Brixton. Two characters in the first of Scott's 'Raj Quartet' of novels particularly embody this theme.

Miss Crane, a middle-aged spinster who came to India as a governess, and became an untrained teacher, could not break through the prickly reserve of her young Indian colleague, Mr Chaudhuri: an 'unsympathetic silence . . . always fell directly she and Mr Chaudhuri were alone.'[1] Cut off together in a remote village by the outbreak of rioting, they began a journey back towards the town. Miss Crane had the feeling that

. . . she was about to go over the hump thirty-five years of effort and willingness had never really got her over; the hump, however high or low it was, which, however hard you tried, still lay in the path of thoughts you sent flowing out to a man or woman whose skin was of a different colour from your own. Were it only the size of a pebble, the hump was always there, disrupting the purity of that flow, the purity of the thoughts.[2]

On the road, they are stopped by rioters, Mr Chaudhuri is beaten to death, and Miss Crane – bruised but intact – sits weeping and holding his hand until the authorities arrive. Later, increasingly exhausted and distracted, she reflects that

For years, for nearly a century, the books that Indians have read have been the books of our English radicals, our English liberals. There has been, you see, a seed. A seed planted in the Indian imagination and in the English imagination. Out of it was to come something sane and grave, full of dignity, full of thoughtfulness and kindness and peace and wisdom. . . . For years we have been promising and for years finding means of putting the fulfilment of the promise off until the promise stopped looking like a promise and started looking only like a sinister prevarication, even to me, let alone to Indians who think and feel and know the same as me. And the tragedy is that between us there is this little matter of the colour of the skin which gets in the way of our seeing through each other's failings and seeing into each other's hearts. Because if we saw through *them*, and into *them* then we should know. And what we should know is that a promise is a promise and will be fulfilled.[3]

Daphne Manners, in her twenties, niece of the Governor of the province, was out of sympathy with the ethos of the British social set. She struck up a friendship with Hari

Kumar, an embittered ex-public school Indian who had been left penniless after his father's suicide. At a certain point in their relationship, she identified the sexual taboo as the test of her authenticity:

> This is when I knew that I really loved Hari, and wanted him near me all the time, and also when I began to be afraid for him . . . . I felt as if they saw my affair with Hari as the logical but terrifying end of the attempt they had all made to break out of their separate little groups and learn how to live together – terrifying because even they couldn't face with equanimity the breaking of the most fundamental law of all – that although a white man could make love to a black girl, the black man and white girl association was still taboo.[4]

In Daphne's mind, the issue of her relationship with Hari was inextricably connected with the moral status of British rule in India, based as it was on white superiority.

> I thought that the whole bloody affair of *us* in India had reached flash point. It was bound to because it was based on a violation. Perhaps at one time there was a moral as well as a physical force at work. But the moral thing had gone sour. Has gone sour. Our faces reflect the sourness. The women look worse than the men because consciousness of physical superiority is unnatural to us. A white man in India can feel physically superior without unsexing himself. But what happens to a woman if she tells herself that ninety-nine per cent of the men she sees are not men at all, but creatures of an inferior species whose colour is their main distinguishing mark? What happens when you unsex a nation, treat it like a nation of eunuchs? Because that's what we've done isn't it?[5]

What these examples show is the collapse of the moral order on which privileged benevolence was based, and a fundamental loss of confidence amongst the 'superior' class or race about their position in the social order. Much the same fate overtook social work in Britain in the inter-war period. The principles governing Victorian social work were taken to be universal moral values, which applied to all kinds of social conduct. New insights from the social sciences, from a new literary consciousness, and from the developing political consciousness of the working class, challenged that assumption.

On the one hand, standards of behaviour were not absolute and timeless. Young people of all classes demanded liberation from constraining social and sexual roles. Socialists drew attention to working-class values – solidarity, collectivism, generosity, hedonism, co-operation – and proclaimed them to be different from, and better than, the middle-class virtues of abstinence, thrift, industry, individualism and competition. On the other hand, fears of a revolutionary overthrow of the social order made the middle classes, from which social workers had been drawn, more defensive, more self-conscious, and more conservative. There was more emphasis on the need for social discipline and social duty, on the dangers of giving too much power and independence of action to the lower orders, and on their capacity for self-destructive folly.

For the Victorians, client self-determination was an absolute standard. People must be free to choose their own destinies, to make what they would of their lives by their own decisions. By the 1920s this principle had been considerably modified. People were not, in any case, free agents. Much of their behaviour was shaped by unseen psychological and social forces. They could not be assumed to be free to choose rationally or wisely. Self-determination became a *psychological aim* rather than an overriding principle. Work should be aimed at helping 'free' people from the irrational psychological forces or cultural blinkers that limited their capacities for true choice. People were not reliably responsible or clear-minded until they had undergone a process of guidance and change. In the meantime, they should be to some extent protected from the consequences of their decisions, and to some extent reminded of or forced to recognize their duties to others and to society. So the notion of 'client self-determination' came to mean that clients should be allowed to make choices, but only once they were deemed capable of making 'sound' choices – sound by the (predominantly middle-class, conservative) standards of their social workers.

Hence there came to be a kind of mental split in the theory of social work. On the one hand, new approaches were advocated which incorporated psychological insights and techniques. Within the entirely artificial environment – the social vacuum – of the therapeutic session, they advocated a radical form of ethical neutrality and permissiveness. During the counselling hour, anything went; the client could pour out all his malice, spite, destructive wish-fulfilment, anti-social impulses, without fear of resistance or contradiction, so long as this was all in the realms of fantasy.

On the other hand, some branches of social work became more firmly identified with law-enforcement and the inculcation of social conformity. Certain client groups were seen as requiring prolonged protection or training. In these branches of work (particularly in residential establishments) the uses of psychological manipulation and authoritative control came to be allowed. And above all, social workers in state agencies, with legal powers and duties, began to grow in numbers, while their counterparts in voluntary organizations declined.

During the transitional period which began with the First World War, the new boundaries of social work ethics were by no means clear. One victim of the professional confusion of this era – indeed a deviant who served to define these boundaries more clearly – was the American educationalist, Homer Lane. Lane came to England just before the First World War, and started a school for difficult adolescents (which was granted a Home Office certificate) run on the lines of a democratic republic. His original guiding principles were moral and political, making the children responsible both individually and collectively for their actions, and showing that they responded positively to the challenges this gave them. However, during the war he was increasingly influenced by Freudian ideas, and his political principles yielded to psychological techniques. When he was accused by some of his female pupils of sexual assaults, he explained their allegations in terms of transference feelings and attention-seeking. The Home Office were unconvinced, and closed the school. Lane turned to private individual psychotherapy, but soon afterwards was once more accused of malpractice and sexual irregularities. Again, he attempted to defend himself in terms of the fantasy life of his patients, and its importance to the therapeutic process; but when suspicious financial transactions were revealed, he was forced to leave the country, and died soon afterwards. Lane's career served as a double warning to practitioners of the newest styles of social work. It showed the dangers of mixing psychotherapy with traditional forms of residential care and training and of offering new techniques to the mentally deranged.

THE PSYCHOLOGICAL APPROACH

Between the wars, psychological approaches to social work developed much more rapidly in the USA than in Britain. This was mainly because private counselling and psychotherapy became widespread there, as middle-class individuals became willing to pay for sessions in which they could air their emotional problems. As training in counselling developed, so voluntary social work agencies employed more and more workers with knowledge of psychological techniques. Only in the public welfare agencies, staffed by local authority employees, were social workers largely unaffected by these new theoretical developments. Hence the split between psychological and authoritarian approaches in the USA was mainly along the lines of private and public services, and reflected the different social class backgrounds of their respective clienteles.

As psychotherapists became more sophisticated and confident, they gradually emerged – through their professional literature, and then through more popularized publications – as a new kind of 'perfect friend'. Within the confines of their consulting rooms and clinics, they offered opportunities for the most fragile or fractured personalities to be reinforced or reassembled, through the expression of innermost fears, fantasies and feelings. They too were teachers of a sort, but they allowed their patients to learn of themselves through emotional catharsis and the liberation of repressed ideas, rather than through precept or advice. Their form of friendship was quite unlike its counterpart in the normal social context; it lay in the creation of a special kind of empathy, security and trust, in which all things were permissible, and even the most anti-social emotions could be expressed.

One example of this sort of relationship was contained in the book *Dibs: In Search of Self* by Virginia Axline, first published in the 1960s, but reflecting a style of work developed in the 1940s. Dibs was the five-year-old son of wealthy parents, neglected by his intellectual, work-obsessed father, and rejected by his defensive and fastidious mother, often locked in his room for days on end. He was referred to the author's clinic, labelled as retarded and possibly autistic, by his parents, but perceived by his kindergarten school teachers as having greater potential. When Miss Axline first saw Dibs in the school playground:

He walked off to a remote corner, picked up a little stick, squatted down and scratched it back and forth in the dirt. Back and forth. Back and forth. Making little grooves in the dirt. Not looking at anyone. . . . Hunched over this lonely activity. Silent. Withdrawn. Remote.[6]

Her method of treatment for Dibs was extremely simple. She observed him at play in her playroom for some 20 weekly sessions of an hour each. She reflected back to him his observations and comments, like a mirror, confirming, repeating, always neutral. Her materials were toys, a dolls' house, some dolls and small figures, building blocks, sand, paints. As to the room itself:

There was nothing about the room or the materials in it that would tend to restrain the activities of a child. Nothing seemed to be either too fragile or too good to touch or knock about. The room provided space and some materials that might lend themselves to the emergence of the personalities of the children who might spend some time there. The ingredients of experience would make the room uniquely different for each child. Here a child might search the silence for old sounds, shout out his discoveries of a self momentarily captured, and so escape from the prison of his uncertainties, anxieties and fears. He brings into this room the impact of all the shapes and sounds and colours and movements, and rebuilds his world, reduced to a size he can handle.[7]

Initially, Dibs's speech was flat and fragmented; he seldom referred to himself in the first person, expressed feelings or recognized relationships. But in his paintings and play he conveyed passionate emotion – terror, rage, triumph – and gradually he used words which corresponded with these activities, displaying remarkable sophistication and perception, as when he described some toy soldiers as 'staggered by their joy. These soldiers are unloading freedom and unlocking all the doors!'[8] Soon, too, his play expressed feelings about his family relationships:

He flopped down on the floor and arranged the soldiers. . . . He looked at them, carefully. He held one out toward me.

'This is Papa', he said, identifying it.

'Oh? That one is Papa, is it?' I remarked, casually.

'Yes', he replied. he stood it on the floor in front of him, shut his fist, knocked it over, stood it up, knocked it over with his fist. He repeated this several times. Then he looked at me. 'Four more minutes left?' he asked.

'That's right', I said, glancing at my watch. 'Four more minutes left.'[9]

Much of Dibs's play, and the talk that accompanied it, was violent and full of hate, especially for his father, who humiliated him and locked him up. At one point, he recited a poem of his own to a jar of red paint.

'Oh red, angry paint
Oh paint that scowls.
Oh blood so red.
Oh hate. Oh mad. Oh fear.
Oh noisy fights and smeary red.
Oh hate. Oh blood. Oh tears.'[10]

But as he discovered himself through play, Dibs gradually changed in his behaviour at home and school, finally eliciting new responses even from his frozen parents. At the end of the book he reappeared in a chance contact with Miss Axline, as a vigorous idealistic adolescent, championing the rights of a schoolmate who had suffered an injustice.

There were many paradoxes in this memorable and influential

book. One was that Virginia Axline's methods, though so magically liberating in their effects, were prosaic – mechanistic even. The reflective technique, to which she slavishly adhered throughout the case, could sound banal, as when she met Dibs's mother:

'I don't know where to begin', she said.

'I know. Sometimes it is difficult to get started', I said.

She smiled, but it was a smile without mirth. 'So much to say', she said. 'And so much not to say!'

'That's quite often the case', I said.

'Some things are better left unsaid', she told me, looking directly at me.

'At times, it seems so', I replied.

'But so many unsaid things can become a great burden', she said.

'Yes. That can happen too.' I commented.[11]

Thus Virginia Axline seemed to embody both a technique of scientific detachment and the power to enable passionate expression, to mould personality. This potent combination captured the imagination of her generation, just as it seemed to inspire Dibs himself to deep gratitude when he said: 'It's a wonderful playroom. It's a happy room'; and 'Remember, in here, it's all right just to be.'[12]

In Britain, similar principles influenced a flowering of special schools for children who did not fit into the conventional educational system. A. S. Neill's Summerhill was run on permissive lines, and created a separate world whose norms were almost as different from those of the real world as were those of Virginia Axline's playroom. He wrote of it:

We set out to make a school in which we should allow children freedom to be themselves. In order to do this, we had to renounce all discipline, all direction, all suggestion, all moral training, all religious instruction. . . . All it required was what we had – a complete belief in the child as a good, not an evil thing. . . . My view is that a child is innately wise and realistic. If left to himself without adult suggestion of any kind, he will develop as far as he is capable of developing.[13]

This philosophy was far more optimistic than Freud's; it also had more direct influence on the new generation of post-war helping professions than Freud's more complex and ambiguous theories. Neill (who was a disciple of Homer Lane) wrote simply: 'The only curing that should be practised is the curing of unhappiness. The difficult child is the child who is unhappy. . . . All crimes, all hatreds, all wars can be reduced to unhappiness.'[14]

DOUBTS AND CRITICISMS

By the 1950s, psychological theory (often of this optimistic, simplified kind) had begun to inform the training of most social workers in Britain. However, it probably had more influence on their self-image than on their actual practice. The new notion of 'perfect friendship' which underpinned this theory – most of it American – was of the counsellor gifted with exceptional insight, who understood the unconscious motives behind presenting symptoms, knew how to recognize transference and counter-transference, could avoid over-involvement and eschew subjectivity. This notion made sense in an American context, where most trained social workers were employed in private agencies, where their clientele were largely fee-paying, middle class, and in search of a deeper understanding of their personal crises and conflicts. It even made some sense in the context of psychiatric work in Britain, and particularly in the Child Guidance Clinics, where social workers were co-operating with doctors who were often influenced by similar ideals and principles.

In other British social work agencies, practical social work had few of the characteristics of this rarified activity. Clients did not come to social work agencies to bare their psyches, to unburden themselves of dark fears and fantasies, or to overcome their inhibitions. They generally came to complain about their parents, husbands or children, their bad housing conditions, their debts or disasters; or they were sent by doctors, teachers or policemen who found them difficult to treat, teach or control. Real social work concerned the problems of social, economic and political relationships in the real world. It was only very partially amenable to influence from a theory derived from the artificial world of the psychotherapeutic consulting room.

It was the fantasy life of social workers, not their clients, that was influenced by the psychotherapeutic ideal. In the popular imagination, social workers' status – such as it was – was measured according to their approximation to the ideal of special insight and empathy embodied in the psychotherapist of Hollywood fiction. In the 1950s and early 1960s, a stream of films portrayed the heroic psychiatrist – a strong but sensitive male – struggling to unravel the tortured fantasies of a young and beautiful female neurotic. In conferences and seminars, social workers were inclined to strive for the masterful expertise suggested by this image, even when their working reality denied it to them.

The psychological approach provided a refurbished model of 'perfect friendship' between relatively privileged people in the new helping professions and often still very underprivileged clients. Most people who became social workers still did so for religious or humanitarian reasons, to help others less fortunate than themselves and to try to repay the debts they owed for happy childhoods or privileged educations. Lacking the previous age's social and moral underpinnings to their altuism, they found in the psychological approach a kind, enabling, uncensorious rationale for their relationships, with seemingly exciting opportunities for liberating latent or crushed human potential. It was also an approach which accorded readily with the socially conservative spirit of the 1950s.

Yet ironically this was also a period in which social workers were much more extensively incorporated into the state's framework of social services – a subject which will be more fully treated in the next chapter. This meant that they were involved in bureaucracies which dispensed services, which rationed resources, which made decisions about admissions to homes, hostels and hospitals. They also had legal powers to protect dependants, to control deviants and, if necessary, to coerce recalcitrant wrongdoers. Thus, at the very time that social work was adopting the values of permissiveness and moral neutrality as its ideology, it was actually far more involved in statutory – and occasionally coercive – interventions in the lives of citizens.

These contradictions were ruthlessly exposed in the changed economic conditions of the mid-1960s, and during the social upheavals of the subsequent decade. As the post-war political consensus began to crumble, social work's tenuous value-base was revealed. Social workers had always drawn rather selectively from the social sciences in their training and their theorizing. Just as their psychological theories had been selectively optimistic, so their sociological underpinnings were selectively functionalist, emphasizing social harmony and the stability of the status quo. Social workers saw themselves as attacking social problems and pathologies rather than taking sides in class conflict. They now found themselves increasingly criticized from the disciplines they had tried to adapt to their purpose.

Feminists attacked them for failing to notice the oppression of women, and for reinforcing it with their interventions in family life. Black people attached them for their complacency about racial issues. Radical socialists attacked them for their blindness to conflict and their bland assumptions about the benefits of 'welfare' interventions. Above all, a Marxist critique developed within social work itself, drawing attention to the social control elements in social work, and its function as a palliative for poverty. This took social workers' psychotherapeutic pretensions at face value, and attacked their complacent and hypocritical assumptions. It caricatured the 'reflecting mirror' approach to counselling, which looked for the psychological causes behind material hardship. The radical broadsheet *Case Con* had a cartoon of an earnest social worker interviewing a family living in appalling squalor. He was saying, 'Yes, Mrs Jones, but how do you *feel* about your rats?'

These new doubts about the inequalities and hypocrisies of the 'helping professions' were faithfully reflected in the literature of the period. Whereas psychiatrists were heroes in the Golden Age of Hollywood, they became far more ambiguous or sinister figures in the novels, plays and films of the 1960s. For instance, in Ken Kesey's *One Flew Over the Cuckoo's Nest*, the mental hospital is portrayed as a symbol of the crushing power of modern capitalism. Seen through the eyes of Chief Bromden, the giant, mute, Red Indian patient who sweeps the ward, it is run on behalf of the Combine, a power elite who insist on absolute conformity. Using psychotherapeutic techniques and the patients' own timidity and treachery, the staff extinguish all resistance and individuality in the already broken spirits of the inmates.[15]

In the novel, a small-time criminal called Randle P. McMurphy leads a revolt against this regime, until he is ruthlessly suppressed by the authorities. Although an unsuccessful revolutionary, McMurphy is ironically – and accidentally – a brilliant therapist, for the other patients recover their vitality and humanity under the inspiration of his deviant leadership. Thus anger and commitment are seen as life-giving and liberating, whereas the mechanistic techniques of the mental health professionals are deadening and destructive.

In the play *Equus*, Peter Shaffer deals with the same theme. The psychiatrist, Martin Dysart, treating a disturbed adolescent who has blinded six horses, comes to doubt his right to cure the boy of his obsessions.

Dysart: Look . . . to go through life and call it yours – *your life* – you just have to get your own pain. Pain that's unique to you. You can't just dip into the common bin and say 'That's enough!' . . . He's done that. Alright, he's sick. He's full of misery and fear. He was dangerous, and could be again, though I doubt it. But that boy has known a passion more ferocious than I have felt in any second of my life. And let me tell you something, I envy it.[16]

The psychiatrist expresss self-disgust at his own timid conformism, admiration for the intensity of his patient's neurotic experience, and regret when finally he restores him to soulless normality. In Brian Clark's play *Whose Life is it Anyway?* a young sculptor, Ken Harrison, has been paralysed from the neck down in a car accident. When he argues that he wants to be allowed to die, a social worker (Mrs Boyle) is sent to try to convince him that his life as a disabled person will be worth living.

Mrs Boyle: Try not to dwell on it. I'll see what I can do to get you started on some occupational therapy. Perhaps we could make a start on the reading machine.

Ken: Do you have many books for those machines?

Mrs Boyle: Quite a few.

Ken: Can I make a request for the first one?

Mrs Boyle: If you like.

Ken: *How to be a sculptor with no hands.*

Mrs Boyle: I'll be back tomorrow with the machine.

Ken: It's marvellous you know.

Mrs Boyle: What is?

Ken: All you people have the same technique. When I say something really awkward you just pretend I haven't said anything at all. You're all the bloody same. . . . Well there's another outburst. That should be your cue to comment on the light-shade or the colour of the walls.

Mrs Boyle: I'm sorry if I have upset you.

Ken: Of course you have upset me. You and the doctors with your appalling so-called professionalism, which is nothing more than a series of verbal tricks to prevent you relating to your patients as human beings.

Mrs Boyle: You must understand; we have to remain relatively detached in order to help. . . .

Ken: That's alright with me. Detach yourself. Tear yourself off on the dotted line that divides the woman from the social worker and post yourself off to another patient.

Mrs Boyle: You're very upset. . . .

Ken: Christ Almighty, you're doing it again. Listen to yourself, woman. I say something offensive about you and you turn your professional cheek. If you were human, if you were treating me as human, you'd tell me to bugger off. Can't you see that this is why I've decided that life isn't worth living? I am not human and I'm even more convinced of that by your visit than I was before, so how does that grab you? The very exercise of your so-called professionalism makes me want to die.[17]

These fictional attacks on the ethics of therapy and social work strike very deep. They reflect doubts which are very pervasive amongst social workers. Do we have a right to try to change people who do not want to be changed? Does the fact that they are hurting themselves or damaging others give us a right? Can people ever be expected to 'come to terms' with gross disadvantage and suffering, with loss and bereavement? Is our attempt to 'help' them to do so a subtle kind of violence, or insult? How can we simultaneously claim to be assisting people in their search for a personal identity, and insisting (sometimes under threat of coercion) on their performance of their social obligations – as parents, children or citizens?

The most obvious dilemmas occur where social workers have legal powers to force people to do what they do not want to do – to enter mental hospital for treatment, to surrender their children to public care, or to be sent to detention centres or prisons. We find it difficult to reconcile these powers with our image of ourselves as being primarily helpers and enablers. In situations which involve decisions about these issues, we become self-conscious, stiff and guilty. It seems impossible to combine any personal authenticity with these official powers.

Increasingly, social workers recognize that the standard 'solutions' to these problems do not apply. People's anger, outrage and pain cannot be explained away in the technical vocabulary of the social sciences. Psychology and sociology may help us understand certain kinds of extreme or irrational behaviour, but they cannot get us off the hook of our responsibilities to our clients, and our relationships with them. This is because most such theory is deterministic – it offers us explanatory models which leave little room for ideas of free will and choice, and less for notions of right and wrong, true or false, fair and unfair. Yet these ideas cling stubbornly to the actual work we do. We want to blame some of our clients, and feel sorry for others. We feel justified in some of the things we do, and guilty about others. We need a framework to evaluate our work, as well as to understand it.

Above all, we need a language in which to talk with our

clients about what we and they are doing. This language needs to be simple and comprehensible, not patronizing or full of technical jargon. It needs to allow us to explain why we act the way we do, what we are trying to achieve, and why we think it is necessary. It also needs to allow our clients to challenge us, to point out that they see things differently, and to modify our views. This cannot be a language which is exclusively technical and professional, or this dialogue will not be able to take place. And it must include the possibility of clients evaluating us, as well as us evaluating them. It must allow them to express their ideas of what is right and fair.

Furthermore, it must be a language which does justice both to deep personal feelings about intimate experiences and relationships, and to the equally powerful feeling that people have about the wider forces of society, and their position in the social and economic order. If social workers attend exclusively to their vision of the personal and private world of the emotions, they will rightly be accused of preciousness. But if they concentrate entirely on the wider political implications of their clients' circumstances, they will be dogged by a persistent demand for the human comfort that comes only from a feeling of being known, and understood, as an individual.

Finally, the idealism (both moral and political) of social workers still demands outlets, and if the circumstances of their working lives seem to deny them these outlets, they divert them into other channels.

'Perfect friendship' is still one of these (now covert) ideals. The search for relationships which are open, genuine, spontaneous, undefended and warm continues. When social workers are frustrated in their attempts to love and help their clients, they often turn – along with other disillusioned young people from the 'helping professions' – to esoteric movements for new kinds of psychotherapy. A plethora of these, known under the generic name of the Growth Movement, have come to Europe on a wave which started on the West Coast of the USA. On the whole, such novel methods as psychodrama, gestalt therapy, bioenergetics and encounter groups have been used only very selectively with clients; but they have given rise to great numbers of groups in which social workers have tried – sometimes disastrously – to love and help each other.

The desperation of this escapism may be explained by some of the contradictions we have considered in this chapter. Social workers have to deal with people who are often themselves in the depths of despair, or even past despair, into numb resignation. Although their clients see them as powerful, and they do have formidable powers to control, coerce or punish, they often do not have the power to give clients what they need and want. They are at the lower end of large and complex organizations, and have only limited access to restricted resources. Often what they can give is meagre and inadequate. Even their time is strictly rationed, and they cannot give a generous portion of attention to the client's woes. Yet their agencies dispense commodities with grand titles – 'care', 'welfare', 'benefits' – and their professional organizations proclaim lofty values – respect for persons, non-judgemental attitudes, maximizing human potential. The result is a perpetual gap between aspirations and actualities, between plans and performance, which takes its toll on the social worker's morale, and may lead to the 'burn-out' described in the first chapter.

The novel which perhaps best conveys the flavour of this daily experience of disappointed hopes is *The Caseworker*, by the Hungarian author, George Konrad. The narrator is a state welfare official, who faces scores of human tragedies in each day's work, and prescribes each its bureaucratic ration of assistance. He is called to the home of a subnormal child, whose isolated, ageing, intellectual, outcast parents have just committed suicide in their dingy flat. The child has for years been allowed to go naked, to eat raw food, and to develop in a completely unsocialized animal-like way. He sees that the child is as unsuitable for an institution as the institution would be unsuitable for the child. There is no solution. He decides to remain with the child in the flat, to live the aimless life that the now-dead parents have been pursuing for many years. In fantasy, he imagines his colleagues' reactions, how they would try to reason with him, how eventually they would commit him to a mental hospital. Eventually he decides to approach a neighbour, a prostitute, and persuade her to look after the child. It is not really a solution, but at least he can go home.

As he walks home, he reflects on the futilities of his life and work, but the last words of this deeply gloomy book achieve a kind of optimism and hope: 'Let all those come who want to, one of us will talk, the other will listen; at least we shall be together.'[18]

We will return to the moral issues raised by social work practice in the final chapter.

REFERENCES

1 Paul Scott, *The Jewel in the Crown*, Panther, Granada, 1973, p. 54
2 *Ibid.*, p. 64
3 *Ibid.*, pp. 72–3
4 *Ibid.*, p. 379
5 *Ibid.*, p. 427
6 Virginia Axline, *Dibs: In Search of Self* (1964), Gollancz, 1966, p. 12
7 *Ibid.*, p. 14
8 *Ibid.*, p. 56
9 *Ibid.*, p. 57
10 *Ibid.*, p. 102
11 *Ibid.*, p. 63
12 *Ibid.*, pp. 156, 132
13 A. S. Neill, *Summerhill* (1926), Penguin, 1968, p. 20
14 *Ibid.*, p. 15
15 Ken Kesey, *One Flew Over the Cuckoo's Nest* (1962), Picador, 1973
16 Peter Shaffer, *Equus*, Deutsch, 1973, p. 80
17 Brian Clark, *Whose Life is it Anyway?*, Amber Lane Press, 1978, pp. 33–4
18 George Konrad, *The Caseworker*, Hutchinson, 1975, p. 172

PART II
The Social Servant

4

The Post-War Reformation

During the Second World War, a change took place which fundamentally altered the nature of British social work. It was not a change that directly affected the social workers of the time. They, like their Victorian predecessors, were mainly employed in voluntary agencies, outside the network of state services. It was in these state services themselves that the change occurred.

With the publication of the Beveridge Report and the passing of the 1944 Education Act a commitment was made, even before the election of the Labour Government of 1945, to far more comprehensive social services. Beveridge's notion of a 'national minimum', of a National Health Service and universal social security, spelt the final breakup of the Poor Law. But it was the death of one child in public care that, more than any other event, focused public interest on the *personal* social services.

On 9 January 1945, Dennis O'Neill, a child in the care of the Newport (Monmouthshire) Education Department, died as a result of brutal treatment by his fosterparent, Reginald Gough, on a farm in Shropshire. Because wartime evacuation of the cities had required many children to be boarded out, public opinion was far more aware of the problems of children living away from home than it had been before the war. Enormous publicity attended the trial of Reginald Gough and his wife at the Stafford Assizes that March, where he was sentenced to six years hard labour, and she to six months. In August 1945, Sir Walter Monckton's report on

67

the circumstances which led to Dennis being boarded out with the Goughs, and the steps taken to supervise his welfare, was published. The Monckton Report coincided with the appointment of a Committee, under the chairmanship of Dame Myra Curtis, to report on the care of children deprived of normal home life. This in turn led to the creation of the local authority children's departments, a new brand of state social work service.

There are good reasons why the case of Dennis O'Neill is still worth considering in detail. In the first place, it has many of the features of the modern child care scandals – and particularly of the Maria Colwell case (see pp. 94–6). But in Dennis's case, his death was caused by his foster parents, to whom he had been entrusted by the public authorities. He was, therefore, the direct victim of the system of care which the state provided, not of cruel natural parents. It was this system, as much as Reginald Gough, that stood indicted for his death. The new children's departments were set up in a way calculated to correct the faults in the system identified by the Monckton Report and the Curtis Committee.

Dennis (who was thirteen when he died) was committed to the education department's care by the Newport Juvenile Court on 30 May 1940, along with his two younger brothers, Terence and Frederick. His parents were fined for neglect, and subsequently served a prison sentence for not paying the fine. The Newport education authority had a policy of boarding out children in its care outside its own boundaries.

The three brothers were fostered by a family in Here-fordshire; after a while they were moved to another family nearby. When this second fostering had to be terminated (for reasons that were never disclosed in official reports) an escorting officer from Newport went to take them to new foster parents in Shropshire. Through a misunderstanding, these people had already taken a foster child from the Shropshire Public Assistance Committee, and the escorting officer was only able to persuade them to take the two younger O'Neill boys. Dennis was taken on to another family, who in turn recommended the escorting officer to try the Goughs of Bank Farm. Unknown to the escorting officer,

the Goughs had in fact applied to Shropshire Public Assistance Commiteee to be foster parents. Newport never took up
references on the Goughs, and were unaware that Shropshire
PAC later placed two children with them and subsequently
removed them, considering the Goughs unsuitable. The
escorting officer was obviously relieved to have discovered
somewhere for Dennis, and left after an hour-and-a-quarter's
interview and a cursory inspection. A week later, Terence
joined Dennis at the Goughs.

There followed a tragic succession of bureaucratic errors
and delays, which culminated in Dennis's death. Newport
education department wrote to the Shropshire Public Assistance Committee (who were responsible for all work with
children in public care in Shropshire), asking them to
supervise the O'Neill boys. They did not receive a reply for
over five months. When the reply came, Shropshire declined
to supervise, on the grounds that Newport paid foster parents
higher allowances than Shropshire, and this would cause
embarrassment. Just before Christmas, Newport sent a clerk
to Shropshire, to negotiate over supervision. She visited Bank
Farm, found the place dirty and cheerless, and was very
concerned about the health and happiness of Dennis in
particular. He looked ill and frightened, and there seemed to
be no affection from the Goughs for him. She made them
promise to take him to the doctor, but did not remove him.
She put in a strong report, recommending immediate removal, when she returned to Newport, but no action was taken,
and Dennis died while Newport's letter to Shropshire was
still awaiting the return of an official from Christmas leave.

At Reginald Gough's trial it was revealed that Dennis had
been starved and beaten. He weighed only four stones. He
and Terence were subjected to daily beatings – of up to 100
strokes – by Mr Gough. There was also evidence that Mr
Gough had terrified the boys by dressing up in sheets and
pretending to be a ghost at night. Dennis had not been to
school at all during December, and had never been seen by a
doctor.

Many years later, Dennis's elder brother Tom, who was in
an approved school when the younger children were removed

from home, wrote a book in which he drew attention to the irony of Dennis's death. Dennis had been taken away from neglectful parents, and placed in the care of a 'fit person'.

When Dennis was taken away from home in 1939 he was dirty. He was covered with sores and a rash, but he was fairly well-nourished and he was alive. When he was taken away from Bank Farm in 1945 he was dirty. He had septic ulcers on his feet. His legs were severely chapped, a condition for which he had received little or no medical attention. His chest was extensively bruised and discoloured. He had recently been beaten on the back with a stick. His stomach contained no trace of food. He was dead.[1]

The officials who dealt with the case were working under adverse conditions. It was wartime, they were understaffed, and they were untrained. In many cases, they were clerks who were unfamiliar with the boarding-out regulations. But the Monckton Report repeatedly drew attention to the overriding failure of the authorities to be aware of the human needs of the children. For all the failures of communication, the chief mistake was of insufficient attention to this essential element.

The 'fit person', local authority or individual, must care for the child as his own; the relation is a personal one. . . . [There was not] sufficient realization of the direct and personal nature of the relationship between a supervising authority and a boarded-out child. . . . The administrative machinery should be improved and informed by a more anxious and responsible spirit.[2]

The Curtis Committee took up Monckton's theme in its Report in 1946. Administratively, it insisted that all children deprived of a normal home life should be the responsibility of a single local authority department, so that the kind of muddle between the different agencies which was such a feature of the O'Neill case could in future be avoided. The new children's departments were eventually to be under the overall supervision of the Home Office, the central government department which Curtis had commended for its supervision of approved schools, as the most vigorous and thorough of those involved with children. But the Curtis

Committee's hopes for a new style of service rested heavily on its conception of the kind of person who should be appointed as children's officer. It was 'increasingly impressed by the need for the personal element in the care of children, which Sir Walter Monckton emphasized in his report on the O'Neill case.'[3] The Committee's ideal candidate would be a graduate, with social science qualifications, experience with children and good administrative ability. 'Her essential qualifications, however, would be on the personal side. She should be genial and friendly in manner and able to set both children and adults at their ease.'[4]

The Curtis Committee at no point mentioned the term 'social worker'. This was not surprising since there were other terms given to the few specialists working in the state services. There were hospital almoners, whose role consisted largely of making financial assessments of patients' ability to pay for treatment. There were probation officers in the courts, dealing mainly with juveniles. Their numbers had grown only very slowly since their official recognition in 1908. There were also a handful of psychiatric social workers in the newly established child guidance clinics and in some mental hospitals. All these were specialized posts within the state services, and the generic term 'social worker' was seldom used to connote them all; it still referred mainly to the voluntary sector. Thus, although the Curtis Committee was describing the children's officer's duties in terms of a new kind of specialized state social worker, it never actually used this expression.

Furthermore, although the Curtis Committee was very critical of the lack of training it found amongst those who looked after children in public care, it could not point to any existing training that was suitable for the new service it was recommending. It therefore suggested the establishment of a Central Training Council in Child Care, to promote and oversee new courses of training. In particular, it wanted courses for residential care staff in children's homes, which would teach child development, some knowledge of social conditions and the social services, household management and health care. But it also proposed new training courses for graduates, teaching a similar curriculum, but at a higher academic level. These were to serve the needs of the 'boarding-out visitors', the Committee's name for the fieldworkers who would work under the children's officers' direction. Both types of course were in fact established in a number of centres, in time to provide a small proportion of the staff appointed to the new service in 1948.

The other major element in the Committee's report was its insistence that the spirit of the Poor Law must finally be exorcized from state services for children. If gathered a great deal of evidence about poor standards of care, institutionalization, and a general lack of imagination and warmth in the way children were cared for by the state. It had no doubt that this was part of a legacy of the principle of 'less eligibility', derived from the 1834 Poor Law Report – that those living at public expense should do so at a level lower than that of the poorest people supporting themselves in the community. The Committee commented 'we find a strong impression that the stigma attached to Public Assistance even if called, as it often now is, social welfare, is so clearly ingrained that only a completely new approach will enable the authorities to keep clear of it.'[5]

Instead, the Committee substituted an entirely new principle, which should guide the civil servants who supervised the work of the new children's departments: 'the broad responsibility of the central department will be to see that all deprived children have an upbringing likely to make them sound and happy citizens and that they have all the chances, educational and vocational, of making a good start in life that are open to children in normal homes.'[6]

This was the first and clearest post-war attack on the work of the Poor Law authorities, and initiated the break-up of the work of the Public Assistance Committees, which had been foreshadowed in 1909. The Minority Report of the Royal Commission on the Poor Laws had in that year, under the influence of Beatrice and Sidney Webb, argued that a whole series of new local authority services should replace the Poor Law Guardians. At last, this was about to occur, and the service for children was the most positive and idealistic of the new agencies which came into existence within the local authorities.

Nowadays, state social services tend to get a bad press, and the local authority social services departments have been singled out for particularly vitriolic attack by the popular newspapers. It is therefore quite difficult for us to imagine the tide of public optimism and faith that attend the creation of the original welfare state services. The Beveridge Report, a staid official document, full of facts and figures, and published during wartime austerity, was an immediate sell-out. It is fashionable now to regard welfare agencies as bureaucratic, inefficient and wasteful; then they were seen as the harbingers of greater equality and security, the guarantors against the misery of the inter-war years.

Because we now take these basic social services for granted, we cannot easily imagine what life was like before they existed. In the immediate post-war era, the inadequacies of state services were still highly visible, and the sufferings of the most unfortunate members of society continued. The Curtis Committee's Report was something of a crusade, and its idealism infused the new children's departments. The shabby and jaded relics of the old order were to be swept away, and replaced by a bright new future.

The particular target of Curtis's zeal was the residential sector of care for children. On the whole, Curtis reported favourably on foster care, even if its organization was often haphazard. But the institutions in which children were kept were heavily criticized: 'in far too many areas the child is put into a workhouse ward where there is nothing but the barest provision for his physical needs and where the staff have neither the capacity nor the time to relieve his fears, make him feel at ease or give him occupation or interest.'[7] The Report cited examples of children being placed in the same day-room as senile elderly residents, or mixed with sub-normal adults and the mentally ill. In one workhouse for 170 adults there were 27 children aged from six months to fifteen years.

These children were supposed to be there temporarily, awaiting long-term placement, though they often stayed for several months. But the Report found many of the long-stay homes equally unsatisfactory.

We did find many establishments . . . in which children were being brought up by unimaginative methods, without opportunities for developing their full capabilities and with very little brightness or interest in their surroundings. . . . The result in many Homes was a lack of personal interest in and affection for the children which we found shocking. The child in these Homes was not recognized as an individual with his own rights and possessions, his own life to live and his own contribution to offer. He was merely one of a large crowd, eating, playing and sleeping with the rest, without any place or possession of his own or any quiet room to which he could retreat. Still more important, he was without the feeling that there was anyone to whom he could turn who was vitally interested in his welfare or who cared for him as a person.[8]

It was characteristic of this era that the remedy Curtis found for this situation was a new *state* agency, which would energetically reform services for children, and infuse them with an entirely new spirit. Part of the answer lay in boarding-out a larger proportion of children in public care with properly selected foster parents. But the Committee recognized that there would still be a considerable proportion of children needing residential care, and it made proposals on how this should be reorganized, with many more, smaller homes for groups of eight to ten children. This policy would require the building or purchase of thousands of new homes. The economics of such a measure were never discussed. The Report was concerned with setting new minimum standards in the public services – with new rights as citizens for children who had previously been denied the opportunity to partici-pate as equals with their peers. As with the other reports which inspired the post-war welfare state, principles were more important than economic constraints, and they set out principles for the widening of constructive state intervention.

I have concentrated disproportionately on services for children, because these provide the clearest example of the new attitudes that informed the post-war era. But it was a period of great change and fluidity, in which the ferment of new ideas affected all the services. It would not be an exaggeration to suggest that from this cauldron of idealism, energy and debate, a new social identity was moulded. The post-war public servant in the new agencies – the Health Service, the Ministry of Pensions and National Insurance, the National Assistance Board, the local authority personal social services – was indeed a new social type, a product of the wartime and post-war social revoltion. One enthusiastic writer of the time even suggested a new title – 'the Social Servant'.

This author (writing in 1945) proposed that all these potential new officials of the social services should receive a common training in the social sciences, with university departments as the major training centres. Elizabeth Macadam's book *The Social Servant in the Making* started with a paean of praise for the 'master architect [who] has taken the existing services, clumsily perched one on top of the other . . . and has produced the design of a new structure, close-fitting, simplified, and adapted to modern needs' (i.e. Beveridge).[9] She went on to group together an unlikely collection of state employees for her unified training course – public health inspectors, factory inspectors, national insurance and national assistance officers, housing managers, probation officers, almoners and welfare officers.

Macadam's book is a fascinating document, because it reveals how the boundaries between the different agencies were still being drawn up, and how unclear the definitions of the various new roles still were. Because she herself was a social worker, and had studied in the USA, Macadam made an impassioned plea for the widening of the term 'social worker' to embrace all these 'social servants' – even though its current British use had quite different connotations. Thus she wrote:

Social Work is no longer the preserve of the middle-aged well-to-do spinster and the retired civil servant or business man; its boundaries have extended; its standards are higher and more exacting. An increasing number of young men and women both inside and outside the universities are eager to devote themselves to some form of public or social work as a career, in preference to some better known professions, and recent years have brought wider opportunities for doing so.[10]

Macadam argued that for these services to develop separate training would be wasteful:

Social Services have now no hard and fast boundaries. They cover all efforts preventive and curative which are concerned with the attack on the giant evils of the Beveridge Report. . . . Our former limited ideas as to the scope of social work must be cast aside. Social work is *not* 'welfare', *not* 'doing good', *not* 'case work', *not* even 'relief or prevention of distress'. It extends to the community as a whole and is concerned with all efforts to create throughout the world equal opportunities – physical, economic, intellectual and spiritual for all.[11]

There was much realism as well as idealism in this plea. There was, indeed, a new breed of young graduates – many of them women – eager to enter the public services. Furthermore, many of them saw these services as offering a new kind of career structure which had not existed before the war. They did not necessarily differentiate strongly between these services, and in many cases it was largely a matter of chance which they happened to join. In some cases they moved between them during this period of rapid change and development.

For example, when Barbara Kahan graduated in English at Cambridge she went on to do postgraduate social studies at the London School of Economics and then became one of HM Inspectors of Factories. In 1948, the post of children's officer in nearby Dudley was advertised. Although she had no previous experience or training in work with children other than voluntary youth work she applied, and was given the job. Two years later she became children's officer for the much larger Oxfordshire local authority. When she left in 1970, her staff had grown from 55 to 230 (30 field staff, 28 office staff and 150 residential workers). She went on to become a senior civil servant first in the Home Office and then in the Department of Health and Social Security when that department took over responsibility for the personal social services in 1971. Her colleague at Cambridge, Frances Drake, after graduating also did social studies at LSE, then became an inspector of factories, and went on to become first children's officer and then director of social services for Northamptonshire.

It is not easy for us today to picture the extent of the post-war reorganization of British society, or quite how it was achieved. We should remember that war had mobilized a large proportion of the population, and that the state's own agencies had grown enormously through wartime measures of economic planning, rationing and controls. In 1941 about 10 million people were employed directly or indirectly by the state – some three and a half million in the armed forces, and most of the rest on government contracts (this excluded coal mining, etc.). By 1945 the armed forces employed over five million people. Yet by 1948 there were under one million people left in the armed forces, and unemployment was still very low (in 1938 it had still been over two million, in 1948 it stood at only just over a quarter of a million). Demobilization had been accomplished without the disruption that occurred following the First World War. This was largely because civilian employment by the state remained high. Employment in national government in 1948 was almost three times as great as it had been in 1938, and local government employment had also increased (to a much smaller extent). The war had also brought about a shift of employment away from services of all kinds (especially distributive and domestic services) and into manufacturing industry (which offered more than a million more jobs in 1948 than it had in 1938).[12]

Thus a great deal of reorganization occurred *within* the state's agencies themselves, between departments. The welfare state did not have to draw many new recruits into state employment from other occupations; rather it redeployed some of the enormously increased number of civil servants who had been involved in planning and organizing the war effort, and in supervising the aftermath of the war. Many of the tasks of the newly created social services were continuations of the work undertaken by government agencies during the war. For instance, the new children's departments in 1948 inherited 3,000 'homeless evacuees', left stranded in foster homes at the end of the war, and up till then in the care of the Ministry of Health. This was a significant number, when compared with the 5,000 foster children in the care of public assistance committees, and 6,000 in the care of education departments. Furthermore, the Curtis Committee had found another 2,000 evacuees in children's homes in 1946 – some of the casualties of a system which had billeted over a million children from the cities in country areas in the first few months of the war.[13]

Another wartime innovation which was perpetuated through the post-war social services was the opportunity for young graduates and professional people to make excellent careers in the civil service and in local government. The social services in particular provided opportunities for young women graduates, especially those who had specialized in the social sciences. This was particularly true of the children's departments; by 1966 there were 2,693 fieldworkers in these departments, of whom 861 were professionally qualified; moreover, another 562 had social science degrees, diplomas or certificates, without having attended further training courses.[14]

However, Macadam's hopes for generic training for 'social servants', and for a distinctively *social work* ethos in all the new social services, were not realized. The reasons for this are not difficult to guess. The health and education services already had their characteristic professional leaderships, and neither doctors nor teachers were willing to surrender their traditional professional identity or status, even though both were to some extent modified by the changes in the health and education services which occurred. For the rest, an inevitable tendency towards professional and departmental narrowness, competition and empire-building was compounded by the political intentions of the founders of the services. After all, the main intention of Beveridge, and of the Labour leadership which enacted the new legislation, was to break up the Poor Law, and to establish new systems of social rights, based on new principles. One of the chief criticisms of the Poor Law was that it lumped together the unemployed, the sick, the handicapped, widowed, children and the elderly, and subjected them all to treatments which conferred shame and stigma. The aim of the new systems was to establish a number of separate routes of entitlement to income and services, which would be free of the taint of the Poor Law.

To achieve this, the large and complex system for national insurance benefits was kept quite separate from the smaller, more local system for national assistance. The insurance system was run on strictly bureaucratic lines, with all questions about personal circumstances excluded from issues of entitlement; eligibility was related as much as possible to contributions and to a set of legally-defined tests. On the other hand, every effort was made to distinguish between national assistance (as the one remaining means-tested system of benefits, to provide for the one million claimants who had insufficient income from national insurance benefits) and the local authority services. National assistance was concerned *exclusively* with money, and the local authority services had no powers to give money at all. By keeping these functions quite separate, the legislators sought to avoid what they saw as the Poor Law's fatal amalgamation between an income-maintenanced service based on means-testing (with all its resented implications from the 1930s), and access to such services as residential care for the elderly, and provision for the mentally ill and handicapped.

Thus intentionally rigid administrative boundaries were created between the various services. On the one hand, the civil service departments concerned with income maintenance were virtually immune from social work ideas or training, and saw social workers as a different breed, concerned with quite different problems. On the other hand, the local authority departments concerned with personal social services for separate client groups – the children's departments, the welfare departments for the elderly and the homeless, and the mental health sections of health departments – were constructed around the provision of specific, legally-defined services for their clienteles. It was not until the 1960s that the wisdom of this careful compartmentalization of functions began to be questioned. Meanwhile, once established, these new social services quickly developed different traditions, procedures and career structures. Although all attracted some graduates, and particularly social science graduates, all provided a rapid process of induction into their own organizations, so that changes from one service to another became uncommon. Within a few years of their creation, these new agencies had developed into relatively separate and stable bureaucracies, with fairly rigid boundaries, as liable to be competitive as co-operative in their dealings with each other. What brought some of them together will be examined in the next chapter.

REFERENCES

1 Tom O'Neill, *A Place Called Hope*, Blackwell (Practice of Social Work Series), 1981, p. 68

2 *Report by Sir Walter Monckton on the circumstances which led to the boarding out of Dennis and Terence O'Neill at Bank Farm, Minsterley, and the steps taken to supervise their welfare,* Cmnd 6636, HMSO, 1945, pp. 15, 17, 18

3 *Report of the Care of Children Committee*, Cmnd 6922, HMSO, 1946, para. 441, p. 146

4 *Ibid.*, para. 446, p. 149

5 *Ibid.*, para. 439, p. 144

6 *Ibid.*, para. 435, p. 143

7 *Ibid.*, para. 415, p. 133

8 *Ibid.*, para. 418, p. 134

9 Elizabeth Macadam, *The Social Servant in the Making*, Allen & Unwin, 1945, p. 15

10 *Ibid.*, p. 35

11 *Ibid.*, pp. 126, 134–5

12 C. H. Feinstein, *Statistical tables of National Income, Expenditure and Output of the UK, 1855–1965*, Cambridge University Press, 1972, Tables 57 and 59.

13 Jean Packman, *The Child's Generation* (1975), Blackwell and Robertson, 1981, p. 21

14 *Report of the Committee on Local Authority and Allied Personal Social Services*, Cmnd 3703, HMSO, 1968, Appendix M, p. 336

5

Reorganization and its Discontents

In chapter 3 I decribed some of the traditions that contributed to pre-war social work. I also described the (largely American) literature on counselling and psychotherapy which influenced social work training in the 1950s. As different interest an status groups developed within the welfare state, and within social work, they tended to define themselves by reference to the notions of professionalism and training. Those groups which aspired to professional status tended to develop specialized training, with a rather narrow basis. However much they might have owed their origins to a generalized political movement, they pinned their hopes of advancement on professional specialization. Those with less hopes of such lofty status concentrated on a more technical approach, which emphasized their legal and organizational basis. Gaining their identities from their official roles rather than from their training, they none the less developed a kind of specialization by function which separated them from workers in other agencies.

Characteristic of the first group of workers was a small elite of psychiatric social workers, most of who worked in hospitals and child guidance clinics. In the 1950s, this group most wholeheartedly espoused the American psychotherapeutic ideals and methods, and most influenced – and was influenced by – the kind of training that was available. Their emphasis was on individual help with inner emotional problems, and they were much concerned with exploring the differences and similarities between casework and psychoanalysis. To those outside their services, they often seemed precious and protected from the harsh world of 'real' social work. They could select their clients, and seemed most interested in esoteric neuroses and bizarre fantasies. They seemed also to find hobnobbing with psychiatrists more congenial than fraternizing with their colleagues from other social work agencies.

Probation officers were another specialized group who enjoyed high status. As a predominantly male service with a high proportion of trained personnel, they also enjoyed the advantages of being attached to the courts, which gave them a relatively autonomous professional position. They too were rather attracted by the psychoanalytic views, which dominated training in the 1950s, and which seemed to explain some irrational forms of criminal behaviour. But this flirtation with American theory was considerably offset by the strong representation of Home Office trained ex-uniformed services men in the probation service, which gave it its distinctively pipe-smoking, tweed-jacketed image. It was sometimes difficult to know whether the grunts from behind the pipe-smoke that were evinced by clients' reluctant self-revelations were those of reflective, non-judgemental counselling or simply the exercise of the military stiff upper lip. The probation service received an enormous and gratuitous boost in public esteem from the long-running ITV series, 'Probation Officer'.

The child care service was perhaps the most ambitious and idealistic of the new local authority services, and grew much more quickly than psychiatric social work or probation. But much of its idealism in the 1950s stemmed from its particular commitment to its client group, and against the old order. Its specialization was not so much that of professionalism or of American-style training, but more in terms of its almost missionary zeal. As John Stroud wrote:

There was a tremendous crusading atmosphere about the new service. Our impression at the University was that the country outside was dotted with castle-like institutions in which hundreds of children dressed in blue serge were drilled to the sound of whistles.

We were going to tear down the mouldering bastions. We were going to replace or re-educate the squat and brutal custodians. I had a dream of myself letting up a blind so that sunshine flooded into a darkened room as I turned, with a frank and friendly smile, to the little upturned faces within.[1]

By contrast, the local authority welfare and mental health services were apparently greyer and less flamboyant organizations. The welfare departments, which dealt mainly with the elderly, the handicapped, and the homeless, inherited more of the Poor Law's institutions, staff and residents than the children's departments, and hence more of its traditional procedures and attitudes. In 1958, the vast majority of its welfare officers were men in the forty to sixty age range, compared with the younger, more female-dominated child care service.[2] The qualification held by welfare department employees in the older group (if they had a qualification at all) was the relieving officer's certificate, a Poor Law basic training.[3] By 1966, only 10 per cent of the social workers employed by the welfare services had professional qualifications, and another 7 per cent social sciences degrees or diplomas. The proportions of trained personnel among mental health social workers were only slightly higher.[4]

But even more extreme than these contrasts were those between the proportions of trained and untrained workers in field and residential work. By 1966 there were 5,600 care staff in children's homes and nurseries, and a further 31,970 staff in residential homes (including manual and domestic staff) employed by local authorities in England and Wales. The Williams Report of 1967 estimated that 98 per cent of staff in old people's homes and 82 per cent of staff in children's homes had no training whatsoever. Even more damaging was the fact that 72 per cent of those in charge of these homes had no relevant training.[5]

Furthermore, there were huge numbers of other untrained workers in hostels and training centres for the mentally subnormal (over 4,000) in day nurseries (over 5,000), in education welfare (over 2,000) and above all working as home helps (over 30,000).[6] Each of these branches of the personal social services had developed in an *ad hoc* way, with its own ethos and style, but without systematic planning or scientific method.

The 1950s and 1960s were a period of steady growth in expenditure on the social services – only in housing did spending fall for a time, though it grew rapidly again in the later 1960s. Each of the services developed a kind of growth momentum of its own. Their expansion represented the development of professional and administrative empires, in which interest groups competed and coalesced at various times. This piecemeal growth of the social services was characteristic of an era of social democratic compromise and economic expansion, and occurred all over the advanced industrialized world. It was particularly marked in Europe, where countries which had had no wartime conversion to the principles of the welfare state none the less developed similar – and in most cases more generously resourced – social services.

Among the British local authority personal social services, the spending in the welfare departments expanded much more rapidly than in the child care service. Welfare departments' expenditure increased by 234 per cent between 1952 and 1968, compared with 127 per cent by the children's departments, at constant prices.[7] Indeed, the welfare departments had the highest rate of growth of spending of all the social services. This was composed mainly of capital spending on new old people's homes, and current spending on staffing for them. The increase was mainly due to demographic changes, because the number of men and women over pensionable age increased from 6,850,000 in 1951 to 8,898,000 in 1971, and from 13.6 per cent to 16 per cent of the total population.[8]

Each local authority department had started with a task that was clearly related to institutional provision for its client group. We have already seen how the children's departments defined their task mainly in terms of improving residential care for children, and increasing the proportion of children in foster care. For the elderly, the welfare departments had a major job to do in improving the standards in their old residential homes (usually ex-workhouses) and building and staffing new ones. In the fields of mental illness and handicap, local authority officers had statutory tasks concerned with the assessment and certification of patients, and with after-care of those discharged from hospital. But for all these agencies, the possibility of *preventive* work arose. Rather than waiting for children to come into care, or old people to enter homes, or the mentally ill to be hospitalized, they might try to provide services in the community, to try to reduce the numbers needing residential provision. Some departments were very cautious about undertaking preventive work, sticking narrowly to those referred as in need of public care; others, more ambitious and adventurous, began to pioneer services. Some children's departments were particularly innovative; Oxfordshire, for instance, began to work not only with families identified as 'at risk', but also with juvenile delin-quents, trying to keep them out of court, or out of the approved schools, by using alternatives within the child care system. Other local authorities argued that this was none of their responsibility. Gradually, the pioneers' efforts in pre-vention were recognized, and statutory encouragement was provided – for instance in the Mental Health Act of 1959, the Children and Young Persons Act of 1963, and the Health Services and Public Health Act of 1967. The narrow and exclusive focus on people in immediate need, and on legal definitions of entitlement, that had been characteristic of the post-war services, had begun to alter.

† In the 1950s also the phenomenon of the 'problem family' began to be noticed and remarked upon. The post-war services were designed for individual needs, but some families seemed to require several services simultaneously. 'Problem families' were characterized by poverty, housing difficulties, educational and cultural deprivation, and their needs for special attention from children's, welfare and mental health departments all at once. Articles in social work journals began to theorize about the particular emotional pathologies which might be indicated by such concatenations of problems. But administrators pointed out that effective 'prevention' might well entail that one department had clear responsibility, and wider powers, to deal with a small number of such families

who demanded a disproportionate amount of their workers' time. In some areas children's departments set up specialist services giving intensive attention to such families, which included a range of practical supports, and even some limited financial assistance; in others, they became the clients of welfare departments, often using similar methods.

By the mid-1960s, the move towards preventive services, and the recognition of overlap between the local authority departments, had both contributed towards the growth of a movement that argued that these services should be amalgamated into a single agency. Instead of a narrow emphasis on the separate needs of client groups, it was argued that such a department could take a much broader and more co-ordinated view of community needs, and organize a more logical and efficient delivery of services. Furthermore, the common ground between the tasks of social workers was increasingly recognized, and the Younghusband Report had recommended new two-year training courses for workers in all the local authority personal services, with a common curriculum. Criticisms and proposals from a number of government reports were taken up by the Labour Party in opposition just before the 1964 General Election, and became part of the policy of the Wilson Government.

This interest in creating a new, enlarged local authority service must be understood in terms of the political theories of the mid-1960s. At this time, the Labour Government was trying to plan for more rapid economic growth through a 'rationalization' of both industry and the state's services. The wisdom of the age favoured the creation of large units in both spheres – mergers were creating giant companies in private industry, and in the state ministries were being combined into enormous new departments, like Health and Social Security and the Environment. In line with notions about the need for better planning and 'economies of scale', the local authority personal social services seemed a target for rationalization.

Secondly, it was becoming increasingly clear that the post-war welfare state had not 'solved' social problems in the way that its architects had hoped. Within a year of the new Labour Government coming to power, researchers were drawing attention to the continued existence of poverty – millions living *below* the official poverty line, including many large families with breadwinners in low-paid employment – and demanding reforms. The Labour Government quickly took steps to change the National Assistance Board into the Supplementary Benefits Commission, to widen its entitlements, and to begin its closer integration with the national insurance system. The new trend was away from *separate* services, and towards increased co-ordination between already larger services. This in turn led to new 'boundary' problems, and increased pressure for still more mergers and combinations.

Thirdly, the Labour Party was committed to reorganizing the juvenile courts, and to removing as many juvenile delinquents as possible from the whole court system. This policy – in which Lord Longford had been particularly influential – called for a reorganized children's department, with powers to deal with tough youngsters as well as deprived ones, and a strengthened emphasis on *family* work and prevention.

By the mid–1960s there were strong pressures to reorganize the local authority services. Critics drew attention to poor co-ordination between the various departments, both in planning and in their dealings with particular cases. A number of official reports had suggested that they should all devote more attention to the prevention of deprivation and the need for residential care, and to increased provision in the community for groups such as the mentally ill and handicapped.

There was also pressure from the emerging social work profession itself for a unified 'family service' which would amalgamate all the local authority personal social services. The main pressure group consisted of a Standing Conference of Organizations of Social Workers, which represented the views of all the major social workers' organizations, but in which those with the highest proportions of trained staff (psychiatric social work, medical social work and probation) tended to be disproportionately strong. The chief point on which they all agreed was that there should be a new unified department, and that it should be headed by a social worker.

In many local authorities, among social workers, only children's officers were executive heads of their departments; other social workers were answerable to the Medical Officer of Health. Although the professional argument for unification was that the needs of families were fragmented between the various departments in the old structure, it is difficult to avoid the conclusion that the chief advantage of unification was a far better career structure for the profession.

When in 1966 the Seebohm Committee was appointed to consider the reorganization of the local authority personal social services, the constituent bodies of the Standing Conference gave conflicting evidence about who should be included in the new departments and how. For instance, the National Association of Probation Officers, though itself divided, recommended that the probation service should stay outside the new departments. The Association of Child Care Officers thought that services for children should be included first, and other services added in only later. There was also disagreement over the degree of specialization that should continue after amalgamation, with the powerful Association of Psychiatric Social Workers arguing that its members should retain their identity and specialized role.[9]

In the event, the Seebohm Committee recommended an amalgamation of children's, welfare, mental health, education welfare, child guidance and the home help services. It took in all the local authority field, administrative and residential personnel and the social workers from the health services, but left out probation officers (even though their Scottish counterparts were included in the social work departments north of the border). There were still illogical distinctions. Occupational therapists who visited people in their homes were part of the new social services department; those who saw people in hospitals were health service employees. Care assistants in old people's homes were residential social workers; nursing auxiliaries in geriatric and psychogeriatric hospitals were a species of nurse. Meals on wheels were part of social services; school dinner ladies were part of education.

The new social services departments, which came into being in 1971, involved major administrative restructuring, and the creation of new teams of field social workers, most of which contained some staff from each of the previously separate services. Seebohm had recommended such generic teams, but had suggested that a degree of specialization continued after reorganization. In fact, the vast majority of the new teams were set up in such a way that nearly all social workers took mixed caseloads of clients from every group. Within the higher management levels, staff from the welfare departments, who were numerically the strongest, and had handled the largest budgets, tended to get the top jobs.

Carole Satyamurti has painted a vivid picture of one inner-city social services department during the year after the Seebohm unification. The new director, a former welfare officer, employed the rhetoric of planning and management, but Satyamurti's research found them sadly lacking in reality:

Every morning at 9 a.m. the Director, Assistant Director and Group Controllers . . . met in Mr Ames's room for what was up to one and a half hours, so that for those involved the equivalent of nearly a whole working day every week was used in this way. The meeting had no agenda, but consisted in the *ad hoc* discussion of what seemed a random selection of the department's mail, plus anything anyone felt like bringing up. The letters were hardly ever used as the basis for a discussion of general principles, but were simply read by everyone, and put aside to be passed to the appropriate area team. Everyone was looking at different things at any given time, and any discussion that arose from a particular item frequently only had the attention of two or three people.[10]

The lack of leadership in planning and setting objectives meant that:

Ultimately the responsibility for deciding on priorities rested with those who were delivering the service, that is, the social workers. . . . [This] meant that there was no clear-cut decisions, but rather that social workers responded to whatever pressures seemed most to impinge upon them, and could often pursue their own individual preferences. . . . This lack of clear direction from above can be seen as partly responsible for social workers' chronic state of unease and anxiety about what they were doing, and the pervasive feeling that they were never doing enough.[11]

Satyamurti found that relationships between field social workers and care staff in children's homes were more strained after reorganization. Care staff felt that social workers were more remote, visited less often, and kept them in the dark about plans for children. Residential care itself was little affected by the organizational changes, particularly the care of the elderly. In this area of work, residential staff felt that there had been an improvement and field social workers were more available and helpful after reorganization.

She noted that other agencies, particularly social security, health and housing, were in a strong position to control their own work by referring people to social services departments:

It was a means whereby they were able to set limits both on the quantity and the nature of the work they took on. The social services department could not operate in a similar manner since, as an agency, they were rarely able to refuse referrals, whereas agencies to which they might have made referrals in turn, were able to refuse them. [12]

Furthermore, these agencies and others – including the courts, the police, schools and the public utilities boards – tended to export to social services departments their problems concerning conflicts between individual needs and responsibility to the community:

All these agencies or organizations, when presented with a client or a customer who faced them with the dilemma, in its most acute form, of care versus control, attempted, very often successfully, to pass on the responsibility for those individuals and families to the Social Services Department, in the expectation that the department would resolve the dilemma in one way or another. [13]

Finally, Satyamurti found that social workers felt little loyalty to the new department, and 'viewed it as a source of frustration or, at best, as devoid of meaning.'[14] They turned to their immediate colleagues and seniors for support and mutual identification. This led to organizational requirements being ignored or overlooked. In particular, Satyamurti noted that specific regulations governing the reception of children into care and their subsequent supervision were often not observed.

Management and councillors placed high priority on statutory visits to children in foster homes because, if anything happened to a foster child, and the visit had not been carried out, there would be a scandal. Some social workers understood the reason for statutory requirements, while others saw it as yet another administrative demand. There was a general tendency not to give such visits as high priority as management gave them, and to behave in practice as though this was an area of discretion.[15]

The picture painted by Satyamurti of the role of social workers in a very deprived inner-city area in the early 1970s was a very depressing one. It showed how much of the idealism which had ushered in the welfare state had dissipated, and how organizational problems had become endemic, both within and between state services. The new departments were large, and hence relationships between higher management and social work staff were more impersonal. Claims about improvements in resources and in planning had proved to be a sham. There were continuous problems in defining the boundaries between the department and other state agencies, and a numerous, needy clientele, particularly of families with children, over whom disputes about responsibilities were frequent.

Most conflict occurred between social workers and the officers of the Supplementary Benefits Commission (SBC). This was because, since 1963, social workers had had some ill-defined powers to give financial help to families with children who were at risk of coming into care. At the same time, supplementary benefits had been reorganized, into a larger and more formal administrative structure, and the number of younger claimants – single parents and unemployed people – had been rising rapidly. Satyamurti found that supplementary benefits officers tended to work as if they were defending the interests of taxpayers, and 'identified themselves with what they conceived to be the financial and moral interests of the public at large.'[16] They were inflexible in their dealings with claimants seeking urgent payments in emergencies, or exceptional needs payments for debts on household items. They regarded the social services department as existing to fill the gaps in their provision, and referred many claimants on to social workers. As Satyamurti notes:

Social workers were in a weak position to resist fulfilling the expectations of SBC officers, notably the expectation that Social Services would do whatever the SBC refused to do, financially, in relation to families. Social workers were angry when clients were referred to them for assistance by the SBC, when they felt SBC officers should have given it. But faced with a client in distress, and faced with possible eviction, and/or a reception of children into care, social workers, with the sanction of their seniors, would usually provide financial support.[17]

Similar disputes occurred with all the other major state services, all of which had developed organizational rigidities of their own, all seeking to rid themselves of the demands and difficulties of their neediest and most troublesome tenants, patients, pupils or customers, and all seeing social services departments as suitable repositories for a broad range of 'welfare cases', categorized and stigmatized as marginal or deviant members of the community. As a result, the new social services departments came to take on many of the functions and some of the structural features of the old Public Assistance Committees of the Poor Law – a residual catch-all for people having difficulty in establishing their rights to the other social services, or driven by desperation to seek residential care as a last resort.

In Satyamurti's study, this situation, and the high levels of poverty and environmental deprivation in the area she researched, deeply affected the nature of relationships between clients and social workers. On the one hand, clients saw social services departments primarily in terms of the resources they commanded (financial aid, home helps, day care, residential places) and of their power to intercede with other agencies on their behalf. But they were not at all clear as to how to gain access to these resources or this advocacy, and had differing and confused views about what kind of approach was most likely to be effective. Some thought they needed to prove their moral deservingness, others to be angry and demanding, others still to show the desperation of their need.

On the other hand, the social workers tended to see clients as in some way inadequate, irrational or pathological in their behaviour, and as being 'manipulative' when they made demands for resources in terms of rights. They regarded behaviour and family patterns which were the norm in this uniformly working-class area as reflecting 'low standards'. 'This general perspective meant that clients in particular, but the wider community too, were often seen by social workers as irrational or neurotic in situations where they were behaving in ways that were quite characteristic of the social group or category to which they belonged.'[18]

This in turn influenced the way in which face-to-face relationships with clients were conducted. Social workers tended to treat adult clients as if they were children – and unreliable children at that – and they did not behave as if clients were of individual importance:

One aspect of face-to-face interaction between social workers and clients was that names were forgotten or mis-pronounced, or got wrong. The same applied to records on clients' files – as if clients were not persons, whose names mattered. Social workers' tone of voice and manner with clients was often as if speaking to a child – censorious, or didactic, or giving the impression that a specially simplified mode of communication was being adopted.[19]

This study was not published until 1981, but it bore out what many commentators had been saying about trends in social policy and in the work of social services departments in the first half of the previous decade. [20] These trends were all alarming, in view of the origins of the local authority personal social services, and the aims of their founders. In particular, the impersonal and stigmatized nature of the transactions, the lack of attention to statutory regulations, and the absence of an 'anxious and responsible spirit', all rang bells with Monckton and Curtis's criticisms of the public authorities in the 1940s.

It was therefore very sad but not surprising to critics of these developments in the social services departments when another major child care scandal broke in 1973–74. Maria Colwell's death at the hands of her stepfather was in many ways different from the case of Dennis O'Neill. She was younger (only seven years old); she had spent her early years in care, but fostered with an aunt; she had been returned to her natural mother by a court order; she was killed by a member of her mother's household.

However, in other ways the cases were distressingly similar, as Tom O'Neill has pointed out:

In both instances, there appeared to be a serious shortage of staff, which meant that the people responsible for the children's supervision were so severely handicapped that they were unable to carry out their duties effectively. Geographically, there were difficulties. Maria was being supervised by the East Sussex County Council, while she was living in an area which would normally have been supervised by a Brighton social worker. . . . There were conflicting reports. One worker would report that he was not satisfied with the situation; another worker from a different agency would report that things were settling down nicely. Absences from school were not satisfactorily followed up, although it was reported that both children were working as drudges during the time that they were supposed to be attending school. It was said that Maria was well-drilled with visitors. She knew what she had to say. Dennis was also trained from a very early age to say the right things. Neither child had the opportunity to be alone with a visiting officer. In neither case could a visiting officer really see the conditions in which the children were living. These similarities are very disturbing in themselves, but there are even more alarming parallels. The children suffered terribly for prolonged periods before their deaths, both from the conditions in which they lived and from the treatment they were given, yet throughout these periods they were being seen by officials. . . . It is obvious from the evidence that much of the distress was *noticed*. In both cases it was stated quite categorically that there was a deterioration in the child's appearance. Maria was seen to have bruises, and she walked with a limp. They were both of accused of lying. Maria's injuries were attributed to 'falling down', 'falling off a scooter'. Many of Dennis's injuries were supposed to have been caused while fighting with his brother. . . . Beatings, poor clothes, jobs to do, false accusations, no treats. . . . Yet to me

94

one of the most awful aspects is that through all the periods of beatings, humiliations, questions and suffering the children were being killed slowly, through starvation.[21]

Unlike Dennis O'Neill's case, Maria Colwell's death, and her stepfather's trial and sentence, went largely unnoticed by the papers and other media. It was when the Secretary of State for Health and Social Security announced (as part of a policy speech) the setting up of an inquiry into her death that public interest focused on it. The inquiry itself and its findings were widely publicized, and the attention of the media concentrated on criticisms of the social workers concerned, and of the social services department.

The Maria Colwell Report questioned the professional judgement of the social workers and their superiors in the department. They had failed to contest Maria's mother's application to the court to take her out of care, even though they had doubts about its consequences; they had failed to have proper regard for Maria's strongly expressed reluctance to leave her foster home and return to her mother; they had underestimated the risk to her physical safety, and set aside repeated warnings and complaints about the way she was being treated. The report suggested that social workers in the new departments tended to be less experienced in specialized child care practice than their predecessors in the children's departments had been, and criticized a tendency to pay excessive attention to the importance of blood ties between children and natural parents, at the expense of emotional bonds between children and those who had actually cared for them – in this case, the foster parents.

But the report was equally critical of communications between the social services department and other agencies, and within the department itself. It illustrated how few of the problems of liaison and communication in such delicate and dangerous situations had been solved by administrative reorganization. Indeed, there were some respects in which the reorganization seemed to have made matters worse. The organizational structure of the new, much larger, social services departments was far more complex, and information had to pass through the hands of staff who were inexperienced in this kind of case. Misunderstandings and rivalries with other agencies, and doubts about the credibility of lay opinions, were still major problems. The report clearly considered that the new system had failed Maria, as a system, as much as the older one had failed Dennis: 'What has clearly emerged, at least to us, is the failure of a system compounded of several factors of which the greatest and most obvious must be that of lack or ineffectiveness of communication and liaison. A system should so far as possible to able to absorb individual errors and yet function adequately.'[22]

These criticisms, and the storm of abuse against social workers in the popular press which followed them, provoked a series of official reactions. Circulars from the DHSS quickly followed, giving guidance to local authorities on procedures in cases involving alleged physical cruelty. Social services departments drew up 'at risk registers' of all children whose safety had been endangered, and instituted systems for co-ordinating information from the different professions in such cases. Detailed handbooks of instructions and guidelines to social workers were issued in most areas. Supervision and specialist consultation were increased.

In spite of all this procedural tightening up, a series of further tragedies and scandals have hit the headlines in the press since the Maria Colwell case. Those that have attracted most attention, despite great differences in particular circumstances, have had one feature in common: the fact that they were known to social services departments at the time when death or serious injury occurred. The media have seized on this to belabour social workers for their incompetence, shoddiness, permissive attitudes, left-wing sympathies and bureaucratic blindness. Deaths in similar circumstances, but where social workers were not involved, have received much less attention. Criticisms by inquiries of other professionals (doctors and other health workers, for instance) have been much less publicized.

Most social workers regard these attacks as hypocritical and unjustified. There will always be some children who die at the hands of their parents or caretakers, simply because children are physically weak and vulnerable, and parents have absolute power over them. Domestic violence can flare quickly and there is no accurate means of predicting and preventing it. The very procedures that have been initiated for reporting suspected child abuse mean that social services departments are likely to know of, and have had some contact with, a large number of families where there are vague suspicions of violence or neglect. Many of these are known through the reports of other professionals or neighbours who subsequently disown all responsibility for them. If all the children were removed from such families, there would be a storm of protest against social workers as high-handed and arbitrary, and of complaints about the rising costs associated with costs of keeping children in care. The differences between families where children are allowed to remain at home and those whose children are removed are marginal. It is a matter of discretion and judgement which children require compulsory action for their protection – a matter for human judgement, which is necessarily fallible. Social workers carry all society's anxieties in such cases, often with little assistance or support, and with few resources. Inevitably, many cases involve an element of risk, and day-to-day events cannot be under the direct control of the social workers and their departments. Yet they are criticized and blamed in the few cases which do go tragically wrong, and given no credit for the many which do not.

None the less, social workers have been influenced in their practice by the harsh opinions of the media, and policy in the social services departments has shifted measurably in the direction of more decisive interventions to protect children. Indeed, this can be seen in a far wider field of social work practice than the specialized area of injury to young children. It would not be an exaggeration to say that social work policy and practice reflects a shift in the relationship between the family and the state.

The ideal which informed the original services of the welfare state was of supplementing the resources of families (by such measures as family allowances and other social security benefits, council housing, free health care and schooling) to enable them to care better for dependent members – whether young, elderly or handicapped – and ensure that each fulfilled his potential. The personal social services were concerned mainly with substitute care, where families broke up or circumstances prevented them from looking after dependent members. This substitute care was intended to be at a level at least equal to the normal standard of life in the wider community.

But since the mid-1970s the purpose of state intervention has been shifting. It has been much more explicitly concerned with monitoring family life, and stepping in to protect vulnerable individuals from cruel or neglectful families. The notion of support or supplementation of family care has weakened, as the social services have come to be seen as expensive and a potential drain on national prosperity. But the need for more controlling measures by the state in the family's sphere of influence has been increasingly emphasized.

This has altered the balance of social workers' interventions, especially in cases involving children. The number of children in care has risen, mainly because children have tended to stay in care longer. This is not because very young children have been admitted – in fact the numbers of under-fives in care were falling in the late 1970s. It was because a far higher proportion of those in care either came in via court orders, or (if they came in through voluntary receptions into care) subsequently had their legal status altered, through the local authority assuming parental rights. Hence the compulsory transfer of parental rights to the local authority is now involved in a considerably higher number of social workers' dealings with families, and results in children staying in care for longer.

Based on her researches into local authority decision-making processes, Jean Packman has commented on the implications of this shift in policy since the Maria Colwell case:

It places the department in a different relationship to families – more overtly controlling, potentially more punitive and cast as an adversary as often as a helper. The trend is exemplified by the growing use of Place of Safety Orders – the immediate and compulsory removal of children from situations of danger and risk. Research shows that such powers are increasingly used (in one local authority area in 1979, a third of all children admitted to care in a period of three months were the subject of POSOs) and this traumatic and summary style of intervention must have a profound effect on all concerned – not least the children. . . . The shock of these emergency admissions is also evident in the comments of some of the families concerned. The social services department is frequently abbreviated to the 'SS' in their comments, and references to social workers as 'Nazis' and 'Gestapo' are not uncommon.[23]

This tendency has provoked a growing and opposite criticism to the one most commonly expressed against social workers. As an example of this in the press, in 1982, in a series of articles in the liberal *Guardian*, parents of children in care attacked social workers for abusing their statutory power, and for restricting their rights – not only to have decision-making power over their children, but even to visit them in care. This theme has been taken up by pressure groups, especially those representing one-parent families, who receive disproportionate attention from social workers. As the Barclay Committee reported after its inquiry into the role and tasks of social workers:

Social workers, it is said, frequently fail to explain the reasons for their decisions, fail to give clients essential information about their rights, and fail to make clear to their clients either the reason for their involvement or the extent of the powers which they possess. It was said, for instance, that a parent might first approach a social worker, perhaps asking for practical help, and be offered what appeared to the parent to be a relationship of mutual agreement and trust, only to find that the social worker had all the time been monitoring the parent's child as being 'at risk' and was now considering statutory action. . . . It is for reasons such as these, some respondents said, that vulnerable groups of people (for instance, single parents) have come increasingly to regard social workers with fear and suspicion, believing that they now have excessive powers which they may use in an arbitrary and unpredictable fashion. Gingerbread, for instance, told us that they warn single parents to avoid all contact with social workers.[24]

This is certainly a far cry from the ideal image of

themselves and their mission that the first 'social servants' held. What went wrong? To unravel the intricacies of this question, it will be necessary to consider in much more detail the political background to these departments in social work. This will be the subject of the next chapter. However, to conclude this seciton it may be useful to examine the structure of the social services in the 1980s in the light of the welfare state's founding principles.

In the immediate post-war period, it seemed possible to imagine Britain's political and economic development in terms of a radical break with the past – a new sort of society, with different priorities and institutions. But during the 1950s and 1960s it began to be clear that no such sea change had occurred, that the basic hierarchical structure of class, status, privilege, inequality and differential opportunities remained. The welfare state had merely reinforced many of these features. Thus it should come as no surprise to us to find that the social services themselves largely mirrored in their structures the very features of society that they were supposed to eradicate.

In terms of income, power and status, the positions of the highest executives and professionals in the social services are almost as sharply differentiated from those of the lowest manual workers as they are in private industry. Consultant surgeons and physicians in the National Health Service are able to supplement their handsome salaries by private work; they have command of millions of pounds' worth of sophisticated equipment and buildings. Nurses and ancillary workers in the same service are barely paid enough to live on, and have only very limited control over their working conditions. Manual workers in the public services are amongst the lowest-paid in the nation's workforce, and the incomes of ambulance drivers and fireman bear no relation to the risks and responsibilities of their work.

In a less spectacular but similar way, the personal social services are full of inequalities of status, power and earnings. The pay of a director of social services in 1982 was over £20,000 per year; that of a home help was about £1.80 per hour. Between these two extremes there are many

gradations. Residential workers, most of whom are unqualified, and for whom training opportunities are still strictly
limited, face the most unrelenting, exhausting, demanding,
and often physically dangerous tasks, in caring day-to-day for
people considered too handicapped, difficult or disturbed to
live in the community. Yet their pay is substantially lower
than that of field social workers, who have access to loans for
vehicles, to secretarial help, to telephones, and to many other
resources that residential workers usually lack.

Meanwhile, as the social services departments and the other
major social institutions have grown larger and more complex, relationships between the different sections, grades and
levels of the organization, and between departments, have
become less personal, and more stereotyped. Resentments
and misunderstandings can quickly become institutionalized
and constantly reinforced within the culture of working
groups.

Carole Satyamurti gave several examples of this in her
study of the Inner London Social Services Department. In the
higher management itself, there was a good deal of hostility
between the different sections. Fieldworkers disliked and
mistrusted management, and only identified with fellow-
members of the same small team; but teams tended to
compete with each other. Relations with residential workers
were particularly fraught, and Satyamurti attributed this
largely to differences in status and power:

Houseparents were nearly always less well educated than social
workers, and often without training . . . there was perhaps an
inbuilt strain in the fact of having the day to day care of a child for
whom one was not in a position to make any major decisions, and
who might be taken from one's care at very short notice. The strain
would seem to derive from the emotional difficulties of being
involved with a child, yet not fully responsible. . . . Residential staff
were in a position of having their work constantly and, from their
point of view, capriciously impinged upon by the activities of social
workers, thereby diminishing their autonomy and control, and
increasing unpredictability.[25]

Differences of class, status and power also contributed to

problems in relationships with other agencies. For instance, in discussing the conflicts between social workers and supplementary benefits officers, Satyamurti wrote:

I would suggest that part of the behaviour of SBC Officers in relation to social workers can again be understood in terms of the tendency to maximize control over conditions of work. Social workers constitute a potential threat to the smooth running and uniform application of rules and procedures upon which SBC Officers have come to rely. These rules and procedures themselves, however, can be understood by reference to the social position of SBC Officers, who tend to be drawn from upper working class and lower middle class sections of the population – sections which, for reasons not hard to understand, are the least sympathetic to families who fail to be independent. This factor is reinforced by the occupational socialisation process.[26]

By contrast, social workers brought to their work an approach which reflected the values of their different class background, but which was no more suited to understanding the needs and attitudes of the people who lived in this deprived area:

Social workers were reluctant to come into contact with members of the community because of the fear of insatiable demands and pressures. Yet this fear was itself based on ignorance of how people thought, lived and worked in the community, which would have been reduced had there been closer contact. Social workers were predominantly middle class in their own background, and in their thinking either about clients, or about the non-client community, they did not have a conception of an alternative way of living, of different standards from their own. . . . In other words, they saw people as having lower standards of child care, concern for old people, ideals about marriage, etc., than their own, rather than seeing these standards as different. . . . One example of this attitude was that many parents of children in care felt very much ashamed of going to visit a child if they were not taking him/her a present, and might even opt to postpone the visit if they could not afford to buy a present, rather than turning up without one. In each of these instances that I come across, the social worker reacted to it as irresponsibility on the parents' part, and as evidence that they did not 'really care' about the child.[27]

Just as the welfare state did not eliminate class, status, and inequality of power in British society, so state social work did not eliminate the problems of the privilege and class background of the social worker in the social work relationship. It is therefore not surprising that middle-class social workers still worried about the same issues, and found the same solutions to them, as their Victorian predecessors in the voluntary services. Satyamurti noted:

Like their nineteenth-century counterparts, Urbington social workers (and their employers) experienced a dilemma over the question of the possible effects on the rest of the population if one, for instance, paid the rent or the electricity arrears of clients. In a discussion about the extent to which the community could be expected to give support to its weaker members, it was this kind of perspective that led one experienced worker to say that the opposite tendency was the case, and that one 'problem family' in a respectable block dragged down the standards of the respectable families, rather than raising the standards of the 'problem family'.[28]

Thus the 'social servants' of the post-war period came to reflect some very traditional attitudes towards the 'undeserving poor' and their neighbours. This was hardly surprising. British society had not changed fundamentally, but the social services had provided one outlet for a characteristically post-war development. Male industrial employment grew only slowly, and after 1966 started to fall; it has fallen ever since. Female employment in services has grown much more rapidly and the growth continued until 1979. The social services provided opportunities for women employees at every level. Social work attracted women graduates into management and professional posts. It also attracted local, working-class women, without formal education, into posts as residential care assistants, domestics in old people's homes and children's homes, day-care staff, and home helps. The latter posts far outnumbered the former, and expanded most rapidly in the period 1969–73.

Thus the characteristic social services department employee by 1979 was not a qualified professional social worker but a female part-time care assistant, domestic, or home help. Just as most capital expenditure went on residential homes for old people, so most current spending went on the wages of these unqualified staff. When cuts came, first in 1976 and then, more harshly, after 1979, these were the first people to suffer – along with the recipients of the services. But to analyse how and why these cuts were made, we must consider the politics of social work.

REFERENCES

1 John Stroud, *The Shorn Lamb*, Longmans, 1960, p. 8
2 *Report of the Working Party on Social Workers in the Local Authority Health and Welfare Services*, HMSO, 1959, table 6, p. 89
3 *Ibid.*, table 9, p. 97
4 *Report of the Committee on Local Authority and Allied Personal Social Services*, 1968, Appendix M, p. 336
5 *Report of the Williams Committee on Staffing of Residential Homes*, Allen and Unwin, 1967, quoted in *Report of Committee on Local Authority and Allied Personal Social Services*, p. 173
6 *Ibid.*, Appendix L, p. 329
7 Phoebe Hall, *Reforming the Welfare: The Politics of Change in the Personal Social Services*, Heinemann, 1976, table 1, p. 8
8 *Ibid.*, pp. 8–9
9 *Ibid.*, pp. 48–9
10 Carole Satyamurti, *Occupational Survival: The Case of the Local Authority Social Worker*, Blackwell (Practice of Social Work Series), 1981, p. 31
11 *Ibid.*, p. 32
12 *Ibid.*, p. 105
13 *Ibid.*, p. 108
14 *Ibid.*, p. 35
15 *Ibid.*, p. 36
16 *Ibid.*, p. 87
17 *Ibid.*, p. 89
18 *Ibid.*, p. 133
19 *Ibid.*, pp. 152–3
20 See, for instance, Bill Jordan, *Poor Parents: Social Policy and The Cycle of Deprivation*, Routledge & Kegan Paul, 1974, and *Freedom and the Welfare State*, Routledge & Kegan Paul, 1976
21 Tom O'Neill, *A Place Called Hope*, pp. ix–xi
22 *Report of the Committee of Inquiry into the care and supervision*

provided in relation to Maria Colwell, Department of Health and Social Security, HMSO, 1974, para. 240

23 Jean Packman, *The Child's Generation: Child Care Policy in Britain* (2nd edn) Blackwell & Robertson, 1981, pp. 183–4

24 *Report on the Role and Tasks of Social Workers*, Bedford Square Press, 1982, paras 12.45 and 12.49, pp. 188–9

25 Satyamurti, *Occupational Survival*, pp. 81, 83

26 *Ibid.*, p. 88

27 *Ibid.*, pp. 132–3

28 *Ibid.*, pp. 133–4

PART III
The Political Animal

6

Agitators and Agents of Control

One of the commonest complaints against present day social workers in Britain is that they are 'too political'. This complaint usually stems from social workers' efforts to draw attention to the plight of particular groups within their local communities, or to the consequences of their agencies' policies. Such actions offend people who think that social workers should be occupied in implementing policies without question – pacifying and socializing angry minorities, not stirring them to protest. According to this view, social workers should be seen to be officials who are outside or above politics, rather than protagonists in political conflict.

In this chapter I shall suggest that such a view misunderstands the nature of social work, the way social services have emerged, and the role of social workers. Social services are not humanitarian products of great philanthropists, nor are they exempt from political dispute. Social workers and their clients are directly affected by political decisions, and can exert some influence on policy-makers. Social work raises issues about the role of the state, and the relationships between officials and citizens, which are part of the agenda of every encounter with their clients, and every discussion with their employers.

To analyse these issues we need to consider the place of social work in social policy. But first we need to consider the even wider question of the place of social policy in the political life of modern societies. Why did welfare states develop, not only in Britain, but also all over Europe in the post-war era, and to a lesser extent even in the USA and Japan? And why has fierce dispute about the social services reappeared as a feature of political life in all these countries in recent years?

In the post-war era, the emergence of the British welfare state was claimed as the achievement of universal minimum standards of social provision, and of a guarantee of equal opportunity for all citizens. All political parties claimed some share of the credit for this achievement, and although the original principles of the welfare state were eroded or modified in the 1950s and 1960s, no party attempted a radical attack on the social services. Thus the essentially political quality of the welfare state's creation was largely obscured. Students of social policy were encouraged, for instance by Penelope Hall in her book *The Social Services of Modern England*, to see the welfare state as: 'the outcome of the application of certain fundamental beliefs about the value of people as people and the significance of their relationships with each other.'[1]

A much more sophisticated version of a similar point of view was put forward by Professor T. H. Marshall in his famous lectures on 'Citizenship and Social Class'. He argued that until the creation of the welfare state, public assistance was often confined to people treated as less than full citizens, and entailed loss of civil and political rights. But the new social services incorporated social rights into citizenship, and contributed to:

a general enrichment of the concrete substance of civilized life, a general reduction of risk and insecurity, an equalization between the more and less fortunate at all levels – between the healthy and the sick, the employed and the unemployed, the old and the active, the bachelor and the father of a large family. Equalisation is not so much between classes as between individuals within a population which is now treated for this purpose as though it were one class. Equality of status is more important than equality of income.[2]

Such views tended to portray the social services as having gradually emerged through the application of humanitarian ethics to public administration. In fact, of course, they were the product of political struggle. As early as 1918, the Labour Party had published a pamphlet which laid down the basic principles which were to inform the post-war welfare state. *Labour and the New Social Order*, which was largely the work of Sidney Webb, set out quite clearly a political programme and social policy objectives:

The universal enforcement of a national minimum

The first principle of the Labour Party – in significant contrast with those of the Capitalist System, whether expressed by the Liberal or by the Conservative Party – is the securing to every member of the community, in good times and bad alike (and not only to the strong and able, the well-born or the fortunate), all of the requisites of healthy life and worthy citizenship. . . .

Social insurance against unemployment

In so far as the Government fails to prevent unemployment – whenever it finds it impossible to discover for any willing worker, man or woman, a suitable situation at the Standard Rate – the Labour Party holds that the Government must, in the interests of the community as a whole; provide him or her with adequate maintenance. . . .[3]

The pamphlet also called for 'a systematic reorganization of the whole educational system', the 'decent housing of the whole of the population' and the abolition of the Poor Law.[4] While it was true that many leaders of the Labour Party were by no means enthusiastic about these proposals (as the events of 1931 proved), this programme of reforms remained part of the aspiration of Labour throughout the inter-war years. It was vigorously resisted by both the other major parties. The Conservatives, who were in power for most of that period, skilfully made some concessions in a number of fields, but ensured that no radical reorganization of the social services occurred.

Yet it would be a great over-simplification to see the emergence of the welfare state as a triumph of the Labour

Party, or the principles that underpinned it as necessarily socialist ones. The greatest single influence on its eventual form was undoubtedly Beveridge, who was a Liberal; and the greatest influence on Beveridge was Keynes, another Liberal, whose economic prescriptions were widely seen as an alternative to socialism – a way to cure capitalism of its inter-war sickness. Although the post-war Conservative Party fought against many of the details of the welfare state legislation, it did not dismantle the services once they were established, and indeed consolidated them. Two of the periods of most rapid expansion of spending on the welfare state: 1960–64 and 1971–74, were periods of Conservative government.

Furthermore, outside Britain similar social institutions emerged in the post-war period, both in countries with predominantly social democratic governments (like Sweden, Denmark and the Netherlands) and in countries with predominantly conservative governments (like West Germany and Italy). Indeed, in terms of public spending on social services as a proportion of national income, Britain slipped gradually down the league table amongst the Western European countries; British spending on income maintenance services in particular was low by European standards.

We therefore need to understand how all the major capitalist countries (with the partial exceptions of the USA and Japan, where social services continued to be provided very substantially on a private or occupational basis) chose – irrespective of the dominant political ethos – to develop rather similar social services.

A number of writers have pointed out that the development of social services is not necessarily against the interests of employers and financiers in a capitalist economy.[5] Social services which enable the workforce to be healthier, more skilful and more efficient increase the potential for higher productivity (output per person employed) in industry. The same effect can be created by housing provision which allows skilled or other workers to move to areas where they are in demand. Even unemployment benefit can contribute to keeping workers healthy and potentially active during redundancy. This emphasis on the efficiency aspect of social services contributed, for instance, to the willingness of the Liberal Party to initiate schemes for school meals and medical inspections, and for health and unemployment insurance, before the First World War.

Secondly, the costs of providing social services do not necessarily fall directly on capital. A large proportion of the revenue for the welfare state comes from taxes and national insurance contributions from workers' wages. Once wages rise above subsistence level, it may be cheaper and more efficient to organize social services on a collective basis, through the state, at little cost to employers. Hence the first social services were mainly based on the 'insurance principle' and provided for better-off workers, who could afford to pay for part of them through national insurance contributions.

Thirdly, social services provide an important opportunity for reducing social tensions and conflicts through the state. Since they appear to reflect humanitarian principles and to confer rights of citizenship, they can be taken to be examples of the benevolence of the economic and political system, and hence to legitimate the social order. Many writers have drawn attention to the way in which, even before the welfare state was created, spending on poor relief tended to be increased, and restrictions relaxed, during periods of civil disorder and threatened insurrection.[6]

Thus, although working class organizations and left-wing political parties have sometimes been in the forefront of pressure for social services provision, this has not always been the case. For instance, the first social insurance scheme in Europe was introduced by the ultra-conservative German chancellor, Bismarck; and it was opposed by the main German trade unions of the day. Bismarck decided to incorporate the upper echelons of the working class into the mechanisms of Germany's newly centralized state bureaucracy. The granting of these 'social rights' was essentially an *alternative* to political rights, for Germany was by no means a democracy, nor were civil rights well founded. Trade unionists recognized Bismarck's scheme as an attempt to undermine their power over their members. Later – in 1912 – the repressive and anti-democratic Tsarist regime in Russia

113

introduced a measure of social insurance provision, for similar reasons.

Rimlinger, who compared the emergence of social security schemes in major industrialized countries, argued that their development was in *inverse* relationship with democracy and political liberty. He concluded that 'the more democratic governments were slower to introduce social protection than the authoritarian and totalitarian governments.'[7] He also showed how the Soviet regime in the USSR used its social security scheme to enforce industrial discipline and low wages on a newly urbanized proletariat during Stalin's ruthless drive towards industrialization.

All this shows that social provision can be an ambiguous political instrument, which is capable of being used for a number of purposes by various groups in society, to further their political interests. It also explains why conservatives have occasionally been in the forefront of expanding social provision, and why Marxists and other left-wing theorists can sometimes be heard denouncing the repressive social control functions of the welfare state, or the class basis of its regulations. It shows that, far from being politically neutral in their significance, the social services are an area for political conflict, in which complex struggles for power and advantage take place.

POLITICS AND SOCIAL WORK

If the social services generally are flexible and ambiguous political instruments, the same may be said particularly of social work. There has been no great consistency or con-tinuity about the methods or tasks seen as appropriate for social workers, either historically or between different countries and regimes. Social work has played various roles in contrasting systems of social provision, and has served a number of political ends. Its great virtue – that it is almost infinitely adaptable to social circumstances – also makes it open to exploitation for any kind of policy objectives.

For instance, we have already seen how in the nineteenth

century, social work developed among middle-class charitable organizations, and was based mainly on a Christian ethos of personal relationships and moral regeneration. But this voluntary emergence of social work neatly complemented the policies of the statutory services. After 1834, the provision of poor relief had been strictly limited, and given on harsh and degrading terms, often only on condition of entry into the workhouse. While this served the needs of the dominant capitalist class, by enforcing the twin demands of work and family responsibility, and by freeing the labour market of the constraints and obstacles imposed by the old Poor Law, it was dangerous in that it revealed the callousness of state apparatus to human misery and material hardship. Charity mitigated the cruelties of industrializing Britain, without undermining the economic principles of its new ruling class.

This was because the only passport to charitable material assistance was the demonstration of the individual moral characteristics or family patterns required by the dominant order. Charitable assistance was not an unconditional right; it was given on proof of respectability, hard work, sobriety, thrift – in short, 'deservingness'. Charity thus reinforced the ideology of the middle classes, while providing some mitigation for the sufferings imposed through economic development and fluctuating trade. Victorian charity was useful to nineteenth-century liberal political economy.

On the other hand, as we saw in the last chapter, after the Second World War, a place had been found for social work within the state's own services. Wartime experience and scandal had revealed the need for a personal and responsible approach to the provision of services for children in particular, but also for the elderly, handicapped and mentally ill. But the political will to provide such services had come into existence before the professional competence to do so. The Curtis Committee recommended the setting up of training courses for a new breed of state social workers, not yet even given the name. Although subsequent professional and political developments served to disguise the fact, to make these services seem the product of humanitarianism that arose from the profession itself, this was far from being the case, since

115

social workers in the voluntary sector had opposed state intervention, and public employees in the existing services had been immersed in Poor Law practices. The personal social services were as much a product of political change as the rest of the welfare state.

The form that statutory personal social services take in different countries closely reflects the dominant political attitudes in the countries concerned towards social issues and problems. For instance, it has been widely recognized that the USA has been slow to introduce social services of a universal kind, and has continued to rely on voluntary agencies on the market principle (privately purchased services), or on pre-war style public assistance provision, far more than European countries. Only 2 per cent of housing in the USA is publicly owned, and most of this is deplorably shoddy. Only some 3 per cent of national income goes on state health care, compared with over 7 per cent in Sweden. Where assistance is given through the public authorities, it is much more likely to take the form of services which include an educational, training or therapeutic element – often benefits are made conditional upon clients' willingness to receive vocational training, or to 'improve' their social behaviour. Joan Higgins writes of one programme, introduced after the Social Security Act of 1967:

which reduced the benefits of selected individuals and allowed them to earn them back on a points scheme which gave credit for certain 'socially acceptable' activities such as the establishment of the paternity of illegitimate children and 'activities which are designed to achieve permanent and adequately compensated employment'. . . . Many of the measures taken to reduce welfare rolls were also attempts to control beneficiaries by the imposition of moral standards with respect to their personal behaviour and by the eradication of the sin of idleness.[8]

Such a public assistance system (or rather, complex of systems and programmes) characteristically employs social workers to administer benefits, exercising a detailed supervision over claimants, conducting 'casework' interviews about their family lives, and linking decisions about payments with judgements about their 'social adjustment'. These 'social workers' tend to lack a professional training, other than an in-service induction into the rules and procedures of the public assistance agency. Their lack of training and their attitudes to their clientele contrast strongly with social workers in the private sector, who provide counselling for a variety of problems to fee-paying clients, in an ethos of voluntarism and permissiveness.

In the Western European countries, where social services have been more extensively developed and less conditionally provided, social workers tend to occupy a marginal role, confining their attentions to minorities of problematic cases, where individuals and families seem unable to make the best of their allotted share of state provision. Unlike Britain, where the social services departments are large autonomous agencies, continental social workers tend to be attached to other services, such as health, education, housing, income maintenance and justice. They thus take their colour as much from the attitudes in their 'host' departments as from other social workers in other agencies.

However, there are wide variations even between continental social workers in their approaches to their roles and tasks. For instance, in 1974 Nancy Hazel did a study of attitudes towards the public care of children and adolescents. She found great differences in their approaches to care, especially in attitudes towards residential care and foster care. In Belgium, only 16 per cent of children were placed with foster parents.

Belgium has a long-standing suspicion of foster-homes on the grounds that it is difficult to monitor what happens in small, scattered families. On the other hand, Belgium is a Catholic country and collects large sums from church congregations for children in need which are used to build and maintain institutions. The state relies heavily on residential care provided mainly by denominational voluntary bodies and often run by religious orders, and although there are some small homes in Belgium, very large institutions are still being built. The rationale is twofold: it is easier to ensure good standards if all the children are in one place, and as the care of deprived, disturbed or delinquent children is held to be a matter for experts, it is easier to provide a range of experts in a large institution.[9]

By contrast, in Sweden 70 per cent of children under fifteen in public care were in foster homes, and this method of care was seen as satisfactory. Only 10 per cent of the children had severe difficulties. The number and occupancy of children's homes was declining:

Where adolescents were concerned, a substantial number lived in foster-homes or other small, private arrangements of various kinds. There were few facilities that could possibly be described as 'residential care', and those that there were generally had many vacant places. The most delinquent adolescents and those hardest to control were admitted to the national youth welfare schools. These schools had a 'revolving door' policy, so that boys and girls were placed with families as soon as possible, with the possibility of recall to the institution. In 1974 more inmates were living outside than inside.[10]

These examples show how social workers, all of whom lay some claim to professional skills and humanitarian motives, have their roles and tasks very largely determined by policies derived from other sources – from political ideology, administrative structure, religious tradition, and so on. The point is made even more clearly if we include in our consideration such countries as South Africa, where much of the suffering that requires social work attention derives directly from apartheid policies. Because of its responsibilities for such problems as poverty and home-lessness, social work deals as much with the products of unjust and cruel public policies as it does with those of private, domestic oppression.

Clearly, social workers do not always simply oil the wheels of the social machine; nor do they always uncritically absorb the consequences of inequality and deprivation. Clement Attlee's remark that 'every social worker is almost certain to be also an agitator'[11] has been confirmed by many of his successors. If there was a tendency to ignore this dimension of social work in Britain during the long period of political consensus and professional consolidation that followed the

Second World War, interest in it has been re-awakened since the late 1960s and especially in recent years.

Legislation about provision of services by the personal social services departments was predominantly permissive rather than mandatory, and general rather than specific. It was mainly through the work of social workers that employing authorities could discover the extent of needs, and the best ways to meet needs. While expansion of these services continued, it was possible to argue that the process of communication between social workers and their committees was somehow outside or above local politics. But ever since real expenditure began to be cut back, it was quite evident that issues about priorities in these services involved political judgements. In areas where strongly right-wing councils have gained power, decisions to make cuts have been based on ideological grounds, and the struggle between social workers and their political masters has become most overt.

The politicization of social work really began in the late 1960s, when the wave of student unrest and criticism, which started in the USA with the protest movement by Southern blacks, and over the Vietnam War, reached Britain and Europe. Students coming into social work had often been involved in some aspect of protest or criticism during their previous studies or work experience. In addition, American social sciences literature reaching Britain, and gradually influencing the teaching on courses, reflected a far more radical critique of social policy and the social worker's role. Ideas about participation and self-help among disadvantaged groups developed, and social workers were criticized as paternalistic and patronizing in their attitudes to clients. The Marxist perspective emphasized the controlling aspects of all the social services, and how social work disguised state coercion, rather than eliminating it. Radical sociologists challenged social workers' image of themselves as 'rescuing' children or 'treating' deviants, and showed that social work interventions often led to 'deviant careers' in which clients were stigmatized and isolated from sources of integration and support within their communities.

The critical ideas generated on courses and in the left-wing student culture particularly influenced entrants into the newly-formed social services departments in the early 1970s. In many areas they encountered situations of confusion and poor morale similar to the ones described by Satyamurti (see chapter 5). They were reluctant to be seen as caseworkers, to be identified with what social work's critics saw as a process of requiring their clients to adjust to the unequal and oppressive demands of the social and economic order. They were keener on aspects of the job – welfare rights advocacy, provision of material resources and services – which seemed to be encouraging their clients to push the system harder, to raise their expectations, and to require change. They also criticized and protested about their own conditions of work, and the way the new departments operated. They joined trade unions, and emphasized their common links with welfare workers in other public services, who occupied similar roles – a belated and rather ironic return to the theme of Elizabeth Macadam's plea for more generic attitudes among 'social servants' discussed in chapter 4.

On the other hand, the politicization of social work has necessarily been an uneven, confused and complex process. Certain groups have had an interest in maintaining the stance of detached professional neutrality. These have included senior managerial staff, high-status groups, those trained in the pre-political era, and those with strong conservative sympathies. The most politicized social workers have tended to be the young, recently-trained, lower-status fieldworkers, especially in the urban areas. But this picture has been further confused by the emergence of some small militant groups of right-wing social workers, identified with a virulent form of Thatcherite doctrine, and campaigning for harsher restrictions in welfare services.[12]

What was the significance of the politicization of social work? In retrospect, many of the arguments and conflicts of the 1970s seem naive and simplified; but it was important for social workers to recognize, both in theory and through practical experience (including strikes and protest), the political implications of their position. Social work services, and the social workers who staff them, are sandwiched between those in political control of the state, and their most powerless and disadvantaged subjects. Even if we can imagine the most sincere, just and fair rulers, and the most loyal and committed social workers, the latter would necessarily be employed to try to deal with those most likely to be disaffected and disgruntled, most critical and carping. Part of the skill of social work in any society would consist in *negotiating* with such groups, and in trying to organize at least a truce in their conflicts with appointed authority, and some room for manoeuvre on both sides. These negotiating skills have been a neglected aspect of the theoretical account of social work; they represent one necessary link between social work and politics, and no doubt both social workers and politicians could learn from each other in this respect.

But as well as negotiating *with* clients (individually and in their neighbourhoods, groups and communities) social workers should also negotiate *on behalf* of clients with their political masters. Again, even in the most 'perfectly' organized society, some people would have criticisms of the organization of services and the distribution of resources, and since there will always be conflicts of interest, some groups would feel a sense of grievance. Since social workers would be involved disproportionately with these aggrieved and critical citizens, they would have a responsibility to represent their views upwards, as well as representing the rulers' views downwards. Even a social worker who was utterly loyal to the political regime he served would be failing in his negotiating function if he did not make some effort to convey to the authorities the nature of the grievances of their disaffected citizens.

Yet even this picture of the social work role is inadequate, for it assumes that no direct dialogue between the disadvantaged and their political masters can take place. In practice, modern societies have found great difficulty in securing the political participation of disadvantaged groups, and some theorists have even argued that the poor are best kept out of politics, because they have strong tendencies towards authoritarian extremism (both of the fascist and communist varieties). According to this view, the role of social work would indeed be to de-politicize its clientele; but there seem to me to be far stronger arguments for trying to encourage client groups to take part in the political process, and to enter into direct relationships with politicians. I suggest this in spite of a number of disappointing experiences of attempts at this in Britain in the 1970s, including the Community Development Projects.

In my view, the growth of the social services, and of the number of people who depend directly upon them for their standards of living, and for much of the day-to-day quality of their lives, requires that these services work as a much more active bridge between the world of political decisions and the world of 'clients'. Social services can no longer be seen as agencies for 'delivering' services to small, needy minorities, or distributing benefits to groups according to the impartial wisdom of detached authority. They are a crucial arena for debate about the nature and direction of our society. They should not be a *buffer* between the rulers and the disadvantaged ruled, but a forum for active participation in society. They should not be a medium for provision for those excluded from economic activity, but a means of including people into the mainstream of society. This requires that social workers unlearn much of their professional exclusiveness, their individual focus, and their defensiveness, and emphasize instead existing (but underdeveloped) tendencies towards informality, openness, and a focus on group and community perspective.

My view is not shared by most politicians. This is because the social services were established at a time when there was apparently no such need for dialogue and mediation – when the state was simply dispensing some kind of compensatory welfare provision to unfortunate minorities. Most politicians still hope that the economic order may be reconstructed (in one way or another) to restore that situation. I believe (for reasons that will be explained in the next chapter) that this is unlikely to occur, so that real changes in the nature and purpose of the social services – in one direction or another – are inevitable. Either social workers must help their clients participate more fully and directly in the political process, or else they will be involved in excluding them still further (albeit in disguised ways) from any share of power and influence, and from the active life of society.

Meanwhile, social work's political consciousness is still at the stage of expressing itself mainly in terms of the interests of its own professionals. As resources for the social services became more scarcely limited in the 1970s, political and ideological disputes about policies, organizations, and the direction of change became more overt.

THE CASE OF THE PROBATION SERVICE

To illustrate the complexity of this process, and the scope for manoeuvre by social workers in the shifting pattern of social policy, I shall consider the case of the English probation service.

The probation service is part of the system of justice, and particularly criminal justice. This system is concerned with the identification and punishment of criminals. In modern industrial societies (in contrast with simple societies) crimes are regarded as having been committed against the state, rather than simply as wrongs done to their victims. The state's judicial and penal institutions uphold the rules of property and civil order, by prosecuting and punishing those who break these rules. It could be argued that the notion of a crime as an offence against the state was originally an administrative fiction, but in modern industrial societies, and particularly in inner-city areas, the notion of 'law and order' reflects real fears about threats to the established social system. Marginal, disaffected groups who commit offences against property, or crimes of violence, are perceived as challenging the fabric of society. The inner-city riots of the summer of 1981 seemed to convey young, mainly unemployed and mainly black people attacking the symbols of the state's authority – the police. At moments like this, the links between property, order and the state's authority become explicit.

The criminal justice system relies heavily on punishment

123

for its implementation. In the scale of punishments available to the courts, prison is much the most severe, and in a sense the other punishments depend on the threat of imprisonment for their enforcement – for instance, non-payment of fines is punishable by imprisonment. In particular, prison is the main *deterrent* element in the system, both to individual criminals, and to the public at large.

The probation service represents the principle of individualization in the system of criminal justice. Probation officers present reports to courts on individual offenders, and make recommendations. Only some 9 per cent of all offenders are placed on probation or (in the case of juveniles) under supervision. But a further 70 per cent are dealt with by other means which do not deprive them of their liberty (nearly 50 per cent by fines, the rest by conditional discharges, community service orders, suspended sentences, etc.). Only about 20 per cent go to prison, borstal or detention centres. There is a good deal of evidence that probation reports influence sentencers in their choice of penalties.

There are two sets of principles that can be used in individualized sentencing. The first is the possibility of rehabilitation. The court may be led to differentiate between offenders not simply according to the gravity of their crimes, but also according to their potential for change, reform, new lifestyles, etc. The probation service has always been associated with these principles, and particularly with selecting certain offenders to recommend as candidates for probation orders. Offenders selected for probation orders are placed under supervision, and the probation officer has a duty to 'advise, assist and befriend' them, with a view to helping them avoid further court appearances.

The second set of principles is concerned with distinguishing between offenders as to their culpability. In their reports, probation officers present information about offenders' family and cultural background, education, material conditions, current relationships, etc., enabling the court to make rough-and-ready judgements about how much the offender chose and planned his actions, how well he understood the consequences, how much he was impelled by forces beyond his control, and so on. So, even where issues of rehabilitation and reform are not at stake, and where punishment is seen as retribution for the offence, it becomes possible for sentencers to distinguish between individual offenders' blameworthiness. Hence the probation service often makes recommendations between different forms of punishments, as well as on which offenders should be placed on probation.

However, neither sets of principles have much part to play when sentencing is primarily concerned with deterrence. Deterrence is concerned with striking terror into the hearts and minds of those who might be contemplating offences. General deterrence is concerned with having as wide as possible an effect; hence the notion of 'exemplary' punishments, where offences are seen as very serious, or as becoming dangerously prevalent. If deterrent principles are followed, the system of justice should ideally be seen as 'self-acting' – that certain offences inevitably produce certain penalties. This is the opposite of individualized sentencing. In deterrent sentencing, specific punishments should be linked with all instances of specific crimes. It is characteristic of countries where central authority has dubious or tenuous legitimacy that sentencing for crimes of any social or political significance tends to be rather harsh, and to follow deterrent principles.

In the mid-1960s, the Labour Party put forward a fairly radical scheme for replacing the whole notion of crime and punishment in the sphere of juvenile offending, and substituting a system based on the notion of assessing need for care and control. This scheme, if it had been fully implemented, would have removed all children and young persons from the ambit of prisons, detention centres, borstals and other places of punishment, and substituted child care facilities, under the administration of local authority social workers. It would also have removed probation officers from the sphere of juvenile justice. The probation service lobbied against these changes, in alliance with the magistracy and the Conservative Party. Eventually Labour's legislation – The Children and Young Persons Act of 1969 – was never fully implemented, and the result was a political and administrative compromise, a fusion between the old system and the new one. This represented a victory for the forces of conservatism, including the probation service.

However, during the 1970s, the probation service became more ambivalent in its political identification. The predominant features of this period were a rising prison population, and the declining use of probation orders by the courts – between 1970 and 1979 the prison daily population rose by 8 per cent and probation orders declined by 15 per cent. [13] The rising prison population was partly the result of a higher crime rate, and partly of longer (as opposed to more) sentences. The falling proportion of probation orders was partly the result of the availability of a wider range of alternative sentences (community service, suspended sentence, deferred sentence, etc.). But the main factor which seemed to influence sentencers was a general shift in public and political consciousness on issues of 'law and order', against individualized sentencing, and towards deterrent principles. This could be seen most clearly in the field of juvenile justice where, entirely contrary to the intentions of the 1969 Act, sentences of detention centre and borstal for young people under seventeen increased by 158 per cent and 160 per cent respectively between 1970 and 1976. [14]

In so far as the Conservative Party under Margaret Thatcher's leadership could be seen as the political party most concerned with 'law and order', and with deterrent principles of sentencing, the probation service could not unequivocally ally itself with Conservatism. But nor did the probation service want to commit itself wholeheartedly to any new principles of criminal justice. Indeed, the service had largely resisted all attempts to involve it in schemes designed to reduce the prison population; it had only reluctantly become involved in after-care, parole and community service. Paradoxically, it was the Conservative Home Secretary, William Whitelaw, who after 1979 made the most strenuous effort to do something about the crisis of overcrowding in prisons. The probation service found itself resisting the Conservative Government's efforts to reduce the prison population by creating yet more alternative to custodial sentences.

The probation service's fundamental dilemma is over coercion. Although it is part of a criminal justice system that rests on coercion through imprisonment, it is identified with a liberal and humane alternative to imprisonment, given as privilege to selected 'deserving' cases, and not overtly containing coercive elements. One school of thought within the probation service argues that the service has lost 'credibility' with courts because it has been unwilling to be identified with measures of control and containment, and that it should rectify this situation. For instance, Bill Griffiths, Chief Probation Officer for Northern Ireland, argues that containment should unambiguously be the objective of supervision of offenders, and that the probation service must make an unequivocal commitment to control and punishment as part of the criminal justice system.[15] Martin Davies, a professor of social work and former member of the probation service, suggested to the Chief Probation Officers' Conference that the probation service should be willing to play a major part in

the provision of a non-custodial disposal that will be seen not only as an acceptable option to prison, but as a punitive, retributive and controlling facility in its own right, hard enough to *replace* prison as the preferred short-term sentence when the tariff demands it, hard enough to be acceptable to the public as a just penalty for serious wrongs committed. Such a provision should involve day-long containment for five or even seven days a week.[16]

Against this, another school of thought argues that probation must remain a voluntary contract, which does not seek to impose arbitrary restrictive conditions on clients, and is not overtly punitive. For instance, as Adrian James wrote:

The work of the probation service has traditionally been based not only on providing resources and working within the community, but also on the importance of reaching out to offenders, forming relationships in the context of which to examine their attitudes – to their problems, their offences, to authority – and to explore with them ways of helping them to utilize their own problem-solving resources more fully.[17]

The essential point is that probation is a *social work* service to the court, and should not jeopardize what are seen as its social work principles in the name of coercion or control. In line with this argument, the National Association of Probation Officers has resisted certain clauses in the Conservative Government's Criminal Justice Bill, and especially the proposal for 'curfew orders', restricting the hours when offenders could be out and about.

This political division in the probation service over penal policy seems to reflect radical ideological differences. But in fact both sides' scope for influencing policy is fairly marginal. The faction which wishes to embrace the new Conservative measures is merely reminding its colleagues of a general drift in policy since the mid-1960s, involving probation officers in a series of overtly punitive sentences, such as community service. Furthermore it tacitly recognizes the weakness of the probation service's position in a system that rests on deterrence. Probation is *par excellence* a rehabilitative measure; yet it is to make itself 'more credible' to sentencers not by showing itself to be more *effective* in rehabilitation, but by putting on prison-like trappings of punishment, control and deterrence. There is no evidence that more controlling, intensive or punitive conditions will make probation more effective in terms of avoiding reconvictions. But success measured in these terms is irrelevant anyway to deterrent theorists – prison has an appalling success rate. The control and containment conditions would be no more than a sop to the 'law and order' lobby, a demonstration that the state was not going to be 'soft' with offenders, or to lower its guard in the defence of private property.

Yet the other section of the probation service's stand – on the basis of 'social work principles' – is rather hollow. The proposed powers of containment to be given to probation officers are rather less drastic than the powers which local authority social workers already have to detain the mentally ill, and to remove children from their parents. Probation traditions of social work ('advising, assisting and befriending') are idiosyncratic rather than pure versions of social work principles. Which other social workers (or, for that matter, which other advisers, assistants or friends) compel their clients to come to their offices, under threat of further court appearance, and ask them questions about their lives? This version of probation practice has developed not so much in accordance with social work principles as in line with the service's needs to present a particular image of its own status and its clients' deserts; it has been considerably modified in respect of many of the service's newer tasks, such as after-care and community service – partly by hiving off lower-status or more coercive duties to untrained ancillary staff.

In short, the politics of probation are complex, and have contained a mixture of short–term expediency and professional self-interest. During a period when the coercive nature of the criminal justice system appeared to be under challenge, at least in the case of juveniles, the probation service exerted a conservative influence. But while the probation service prefers to operate within a system based on retribution and deterrence (politely called the 'justice model') it also prefers not to be too directly involved in administering punishments – to keep its hands professionally clean. This combination of judicial conservatism and professional fastidiousness greatly limits the probation service's scope for influence at a time of political polarization and makes it unlikely ever to be a radical force for change.

Yet the probation service cannot wholly escape from political controversy, debate and conflict, because its work is constantly under political review in an era when 'law and order' is a major topic of public concern. The service must resolve its own internal disputes about how to try to influence policy. It must also respond to proposed changes, such as those contained in the 1982 Criminal Justice Act, which required it to exercise more intensive and restrictive supervision over certain offenders. It must also take a stand on government cutbacks of resources. For instance, when the Government recently made major cuts in their funding of probation students, the service reacted with a token one–day strike. This reflected a compromise between those who felt a much stronger protest was required, and those who felt horror at even the mildest form of 'industrial action'.

I chose the example of the probation service to illustrate the political dimensions of social work partly because it is widely regarded as the least controversial and most respectable field of British social work practice. I hope the example has illustrated how even this bastion of the professional establishment is not immune from political conflict and ideological strife, which in turn is a reflection of changes in wider society. But the real battleground of social work politics has been the local authority services.

I would argue that it is impossible to understand the often bitter arguments about the effectiveness of social workers, their proper role or the future of state services without first considering the political and economic changes which have been taking place in the past 15 years, not only in Britain, but also in all the other major industrialized countries. This will be the subject of the next chapter.

REFERENCES

1 Penelope Hall, *The Social Services of Modern England*, 1957, p. 308
2 T. H. Marshall, *Citizenship and Social Class*, Cambridge University Press, 1950, p. 56
3 Labour Party, *Labour and the New Social Order: A Report on Reconstruction*, Labour Party, 1918, pp. 5, 10
4 *Ibid.*, pp. 16–17
5 See for instance Ian Gough, *The Political Economy of the Welfare State*, Macmillan, 1979
6 See for instance F. F. Piven and R. A. Cloward, *Regulating the Poor: The Functions of Public Welfare*, Tavistock, 1972
7 G. V. Rimlinger, *Welfare Policy and Industrialisation in Europe, America and Russia*, Wiley, 1971, p. 9
8 Joan Higgins, *States of Welfare: Comparative Analysis of Social Policy*, Blackwell & Robertson, 1981, pp. 110–11
9 Nancy Hazel, *A Bridge to Independence: The Kent Family Placement Project*, Blackwell, 1981, pp. 17–18
10 *Ibid.*, p. 19
11 Clement Attlee, *The Social Worker*, Bell, 1920
12 For instance, the pressure group 'Responsibility in Welfare', now called 'The Campaign for Family and Nation'
13 *Annual Reports of Prison Department*, HMSO, and *Annual Probation and After-care Statistics*, HMSO

14 S. Millham, R. Bullock and K. Hosie, *Locking Up Children*, Saxon House, 1978

15 W. A. Griffiths, 'Supervision in the community', *Justice of the Peace*, 21 August 1982, pp. 514–15

16 Martin Davies, *Probation Officers and the Prison Service: The Need for Partnership*, Address to Chief Probation Officers' Conference, 1982

17 Adrian James, 'Sentenced to surveillance', *NAPO Journal*, March 1979

7

Social Work and the
Post-Industrial Society

We have seen that state social work services appeared to evolve almost simultaneously in the major advanced countries of the capitalist world after the Second World War. It seems possible, therefore, that they were products of similar economic, social and political conditions, associated with the rapid growth of industrial output and employment, the expansion of world trade, and the emergence of a type of political order that has been described as social democracy. However, since the middle of the 1960s, there have been signs of a change in the direction of economic development, which has upset the social and political balance associated with the post-war era.

Up to 1965, the direction of world economic development could be described as a process of uneven but relentless industrialization. In the Eastern bloc, centrally-planned economics as well as in the Western, free-market economics, the trend has always been towards increased industrial employment. Even during periodic depressions, the proportion of employees in industry grew. Since 1965, the total numbers of people employed in industry in West Germany and the United Kingdom have been falling steadily. Since 1973, the numbers and proportion so employed in all the advanced industrialized countries of the Western world has been declining. In each of these countries, once industrial employment has started to fall, unemployment rates have started to rise.[1]

There is fierce theoretical dispute among economists and

politicians about the significance of these trends. Many would argue that they represent no more than a temporary recession. But others suggest that they herald a new developmental stage in the evolution of advanced industrialized economies – a stage where progressively fewer workers will be needed to produce optimum outputs, and where technological innovations, such as microprocessors and robots, will permanently displace an increasing number of manual and technical employees. The latter school of thought tend to refer to the notion of a 'post-industrial' society.

But these same phenomena have given rise to equally fierce disputes about the role of social policy. In all the western industrialized countries there has simultaneously been a right-wing political 'backlash' against the social services, in some cases strong enough to carry these parties into power. The targets of this backlash have been remarkably similar, in countries as disparate as Denmark, the USA, Australia and the United Kingdom – the unemployed and the single parents have been the main scapegoats.[2] It seems the emergence of a large sector of long-term welfare beneficiaries of working age has provoked the fury of those members of society most identified with the ideology of free-market capitalism. Such critics argue that economic health and long-term prosperity depend on the restoration of the ethic of hard work and individual responsibility, which are undermined by unconditional social services and generous benefits. They suggest that these changes in attitude, coupled with restraints on trade union power, and incentives to economic initiative, would allow economic growth and increased industrial employment to return.

On the other side of the argument, the parties of the centre and the left have attempted to justify the structure of the social services in the face of mounting criticisms. Their difficulty lies on the fact that the social services in all the western industrialized countries were financed, planned and administered during the post-war period on an assumption of continued economic growth and full employment. The slower growth of these economies in the 1970s, and the universal re-emergence of mass unemployment, have disrupted these longstanding complacent assumptions, and caused hasty readjustments. In Britain, for instance, the Labour Government of 1974–79 cut capital expenditure on all the social services, and current expenditure on housing and education, in order to pay for the doubling of unemployment that occurred during its term of office.[3]

Furthermore, criticisms of the forms taken by the social services have come from their clients as well as from the right wing of the political spectrum. Social services set up during the social democratic era tended to be bureaucratic and paternalistic; they were relatively large-scale organizations, which made unilateral decisions about people's needs, and dispensed their services according to their own criteria. They tended to be relatively inflexible and unresponsive to local opinions and pressures, and were unfitted to deal with the growing crises associated with economic recession. When the dissatisfactions of consumers were added to the resentments of ratepayers and taxpayers who shouldered the burden of the cost of these services, it is easier to understand how right-wing programmes, such as those of Margaret Thatcher and Ronald Reagan, gained such widespread support.

In Britain, social work has been singled out for particular criticism by the right wing, and by the media, as part of this backlash. It has been an easier target, because social services departments have been more identifiable than the more dispersed services of the continental countries, and have served a clientele of the most resented and scape-goated members of the community – juvenile delinquents, child abusers, the mentally ill, single parents, and those still regarded as the 'undeserving poor'. Many of the criticisms made of social workers have simply reflected public prejudices against these groups, but they have taken the form of questioning the validity of offering 'help' to such people, and of doubting the effectiveness of social work. Social workers have been put on the defensive by such attacks, especially those centred on issues of child abuse. I have already argued in chapter 5 that public criticism has influenced social work practice in the direction of more statutory removals of children from parents, and more punitive recommendations to courts.

Yet although social workers have been attacked as ineffective and even unnecessary,[4] in fact the importance of their role in the welfare state has if anything increased. This is because, as cuts have been made in the major social services, a larger proportion of people have required the 'safety net' which local authority social services departments represent. Ever since the early 1970s there has been a tendency for these other agencies to export their more demanding and difficult pupils, tenants, claimants and patients to social services as 'welfare cases'; the pressure to do so has been increased with growing deprivation and shrinking resources.

But along with the changes that have been taking place in British society, not only has the quantity of need increased, but also the nature of that need has been changing – and with these changes, the methods of managing social needs by the state has been subtly altering. The old system of large-scale, remote and bureaucratic social services has been found to be not only unpopular but also unable to do the task required by the state – the monitoring and ultimately the regulation and control of marginal and potentially disaffected members of the community.

For even though right-wing ideology denies the possibility of a long-term shift to a post-industrial society, government is faced with the realities of communities in which (at a local level) 50, 60 or even 70 per cent of the potential workforce are unemployed, and many active, vigorous young people have no prospect of a job or independent accommodation. The need for public order and social discipline has always been an important consideration in the provision of social services, and this now occupies the minds of government as much as any other priority.

The problem can be recognized in a slightly different service, the police. In the 1960s and 1970s, the police had developed methods of patrolling based on radio cars rather than officers on foot. The riots of 1981 illustrated the ineffectiveness of these methods in the quick identification of trouble and the quelling of mob violence. The notion of 'community policing', pioneered in Devon and Cornwall, is being widely adopted, not in the spirit of liberalism, but because only a much higher proportion of foot patrols on the ground in inner cities can enable these areas to be controlled. The ultimate function of community police, apart from quelling minor problems, is to alert the heavy brigades (which are being trained and developed in parallel with the friendly neighbourhood coppers) so that they can be called in more quickly and decisively in the event of a riot.

A similar development can be seen in the way in which the personal social services are developing. There are increasing numbers of deprived areas where virtually the whole population are dependent on state benefits and services for their standards of living – subsisting on social security, in council housing, in state education – but where none of these services penetrates the neighbourhood and family networks to influence the day-to-day life of the community. Hence the development of a new style of 'patch based' social work, which allows social workers to move further from their offices, to spend more time in streets and neighbourhoods, to be more involved in local informal organizations.

In terms of right-wing ideology this can be represented as strengthening voluntary endeavour and neighbourly caring networks, but also as more closely monitoring deviant behaviour. For the left, it can signify the breaking down of paternalistic and bureaucratic traditions of local government, and a contribution to greater responsiveness and participation.

THE BARCLAY REPORT

The reorganization of social work which took place in the early 1970s (see chapter 5) did not take account of these changes. Its main preoccupations were better co-ordination between the previously fragmented services, and better planning. It also wanted the social services departments to become major agencies, which could hold their own with the health service, housing, social security, and so on. The changes which came about through reorganization made the new departments larger in some ways more remote from the communities they served. In terms of co-ordination and planning at the level of local authority *headquarters*, this was an improvement. In terms of accessibility to local people, and staying closely in touch with their colleagues in other agencies at the 'street level', it was a step in the wrong direction.

Because the priorities of the early 1970s were in terms of management and organization on the grand scale (not only in the personal social services but also, for instance, in the health service) these issues were not considered seriously. But when the social and economic changes of the 1980s had altered priorities, they were crucial. As with the police, social work was seen as an expensive and sophisticated service which was not reaching down to where the trouble was located. At a time when resources in the public services generally were in short supply, a review of the effectiveness of social work, and the way it was organized, became necessary.

The most recent report on the role and tasks of social workers reflects these preoccupations. The Barclay Committee was set up, under the auspices of the National Institute of Social Work, to look at the future of social work at a time (November 1980) when critics were questioning its professional competence to handle such issues as child abuse and delinquency, and its political usefulness. The eventual Report (published in May 1982) was largely a justification of the contributions made by professional social work practice to the amelioration of social problems.[5] The statement in the Report that many tasks are 'being done by social workers which it would be to the detriment of clients to have left undone' could be taken as representative of the general tenor of its conclusions.

The main body of the Report glosses lightly over the underlying political dilemmas for social workers and for the organization of social work agencies. However, the two dissenting appendices state clearly the ideological conflict at the heart of the matter. Each looks at social work from an entirely different perspective; but both uncover important choices to be made by policy-makers and by social workers themselves.

Appendix B, by Professor Hadley, Mr White and Mrs

Brown, is entitled 'A case for neighbourhood-based social work and social services'. It takes much further the arguments in the Majority Report for 'community social work', suggesting that a true community approach cannot evolve easily and naturally from the welfare state tradition. It argues the vast majority of social work is concerned with low-key tasks, enabling dependent, troubled or handicapped people to continue to live in their local neighbourhoods. Most of such work is already done informally, by neighbours, friends and kin, and social work should be concerned with strengthening and supplementing such caring networks in a flexible and imaginative way. To do this, it should have a strong local orientation, and close links with other services and voluntary organizations, greater local autonomy, wider, less specific job-descriptions, and a more generalist, less narrowly professional orientation. Teams should be smaller and serve smaller areas.

Appendix B quotes experience from areas where neighbourhood-based teams have actually been initiated:

Higher referral rates, earlier intervention, fewer unforeseen crises are all listed as gains. It is also claimed that much closer working relationships are usually established with other agencies operating locally – the primary health care workers, teachers, community police, tenants' associations, mutual aid groups, churches, and so on, and that local commercial enterprises such as pubs and corner shops become recognized as important sources of information. Another common feature of the teams appears to be their ability to foster local voluntary initiatives. . . .[6]

Although social workers have often resisted reorganization on these lines, the authors of Appendix B found that, once this had occurred, enthusiasm and morale were high, and co-operation evident.

The kind of social workers and authors saw as suited to this work were less narrowly professional, more informal and unofficial. Counselling skills, while still needed, would have a less central place. They should be skilled at working at second-hand through lay people, at social care planning and community work. They should be able to recognize problems requiring more specialized skills, so as to call in back-up teams of specialists, such as mental health workers, when they were required.

Appendix B starts the view – often confirmed by research – that about 80 per cent of social work referrals concern low-key, practical problems, which common sense and good organization, together with local knowledge, can do much to overcome. It argues that such an approach could prevent a large proportion of such cases developing into more serious crises, and hence could reduce the number and severity of instances requiring specialist help, statutory intervention or residential care. As confirmation of this view, Mike Cooper – the team leader of the most famous patch team, at Norman-ton in South Yorkshire – has written that his team has not taken a single Place of Safety Order, to remove children in emergency from their parents, in the past five years.[7]

Starting from the opposite perspective, Appendix A, written by Professor Pinker, considers that both the Majority Report and the other Appendix are dangerously wrong about the future of social work. Pinker starts from the premise that 'our present model of so-called client-centred social work is basically sound. . . . Social work should be explicitly selective rather than universalist in focus, reactive rather than preventive in approach and modest in its objectives.'[8] It derives its authority mainly from statutes and from direct political accountability, but also from its professional impartiality and skills. Pinker argues that

Social casework is the fundamentally distinctive method of social work which is derived from social work's concern with helping individuals and families with their problems in social living. . . . The counselling part of social casework is carried out through the use of a professional relationship between the social worker and the client (and other people who are immediately affected), as the means of helping the client to manage his own life.[9]

Pinker is scathing about his opponents' notions of 'the community':

It is one of the most stubbornly persistent illusions in social policy studies that eventually the concept of community – as a basis of shared values – will resolve all our policy dilemmas. The very fact that this notion is cherished from left to right across the political spectrum makes it highly suspect. There is no unitary definition of community because, like the concept of equity, it is open to various interpretations. The idea that in a complex industrial society the notion of community could provide a basis for shared values (and hence for consistent social policy) is erroneous.[10]

Unlike the authors of Appendix B, Pinker starts from the 'hard end' of social services cases, from statutory, official work and professional tasks:

Formal systems of social service delivery developed because the informal networks of mutual aid in local communities were manifestly incapable of meeting the kinds of personal need which arise in complex industrial societies. It is a romantic illusion to suppose that by dispersing a handful of professional social workers into local communities we can miraculously revive the sleeping giants of populist altruism. The most localized system of 'social' service in the history of British social policy was the Poor Law. Its relieving officers and guardians all served localities and constituencies that were sufficiently small to be intimately known. It was just this distinctive quality of parochial social service that added a uniquely hurtful dimension to the experience of stigma among the recipients of poor relief.[11]

Pinker argues that if the community approach were adopted, specialist training would be neglected, specialist posts would become residual, and clients in need of these skills would be neglected and rejected. Teams should remain 'client-centred', but improve liaison with the community, rather than relegate professional skills to a background role.

The political implications of the community approach also worry Pinker. He insists on clients' rights to confidentiality and privacy, and is concerned that the notion of 'informal contacts' with shops, pubs and lollipop ladies would infringe professional standards and civil rights:

According to the Report, this information would help social workers foster a general sense of community, and would also help them to detect needs at an early stage., Not to over-dramatise the issue, a system simultaneously governed by the concepts of community and prevention would be potentially lethal to our civil liberties. In totalitarian societies the imposition of community – in the form of a unified network of local loyalties which are subservient to the state – is one of the basic political aims of government. Democracies tolerate many different loyalties. . . . The desire to locate and provide for unexpressed needs is not a defensible reason for jeopardizing people's right to be left alone.[12]

Pinker is right to draw attention to the political implications of this new model; he is right also to suggest that it is supported for opposite reasons by adherents of both political polarities – the left as a source of popular pressure for more resources, the right as a source of alternatives to publicly-financed services. But he is wrong to assume that his modest, reactive, client-centred version of social work is immune from exploitation by a ruthless political regime. He writes as if the numbers of unfortunates who need the professional help of social workers are somehow God-given rather than socially (or politically) determined. In fact there is massive and growing evidence that needs for child care services, residential care, mental health services, and so on, are related both to wider political and economic changes, and to the operation of the whole welfare state network. If housing, education, health and social security budgets are being cut at a time of economic recession, the numbers of 'social casualties' and 'deviants' does not remain the same, it grows. Hence social work can find itself playing a larger role, encountering more crises, and carrying out more drastic statutory interventions, in a shrinking welfare state – even without any expansionary or preventive pretensions. In the absence of proper staffing, funding or enlightened policies, this can just as surely lead to the development of a Poor Law level of services, and many of these trends are already in evidence.

The reasons why the Majority Report and Appendix B are occasionally naive and dangerous in their recommendations are not intrinsic to their community approach. They stem from a failure to recognize the potential for misuse of this approach in a crumbling capitalist economy. If government

has no commitment to social justice and equ
ruthlessly pursues the needs of capital accumula
expense of people, then the community approach
these ends. But this same approach could give
genuinely more egalitarian, participatory and resp
of social work if it was grafted onto a new
commitment to a major redistribution of income, ···· and
resources, that would improve the material and social
life-chances of those most likely to become social work
clients.

THE FUTURE SHAPE OF SOCIAL SERVICES

The other respect in which the Barclay Report was naive
concerned its failure to address specific social problems and
policies, and to show how they influenced social workers'
roles and tasks. The latter have not evolved through professional and organizational change, but in response to
shifting social and political patterns. The Report did not look
widely enough at the changing face of social services, nor did
it focus closely enough on particular areas of social change.

At the time of the Seebohm Report of 1968, it was widely
argued that there were advantages in putting all state social
workers into the same, unified agency. Before the Seebohm
Committee was set up, there was even talk of including
probation officers – something the probation service successfully resisted, but which happened in Scotland, where the
service was less well organized and trained, and where
changes in the juvenile justice system were more radical. It
was even argued in favour of unification in this period that
'welfare was indivisible'[13] – an absurd statement that ignored
the fact that everyone with the means to do so avoided state
social work services like the plague, and bought the expensive
private services of counsellors, nannies, clinics, special
schools, housekeepers, convalescent homes and companions
in the private sector. If this claim was supposed to mean
anything, it presumably suggested that those who required
state personal social services could be best served by an

organization which planned and co-ordinated all such services in a local authority area.

But in fact, and largely unnoticed, the trend in the personal social services has actually been in the opposite direction since 1970. Many growth areas have been *outside* social services departments, not within them, particularly since about 1975. Some new services have been set up or funded by the local authorities – advice centres, law centres, crisis centres, rights centres, and so on. Some have been developed within the Manpower Services Commission, focusing on the massive growth of unemployment – project supervisors, life-skills trainers, and so on. Thus, far from gaining a monopoly over counselling and personal services the social services departments may even have lost ground as a proportion of all such posts.

Another trend is also evident – the growth of ancillary posts and the systematic division of labour in social work. As proportions of trained staff among field social workers increased, a new grade of untrained 'social work assistants' was created, to deal with tasks seen as requiring less professional skill. Then a new system of training, the Certificate in Social Service, was introduced, mainly for residential and day care staff. This institutionalized the split between fieldwork and these other services, and made transitions between them more difficult.

In the probation service, the new duties put on the organization – aftercare, community service, day training – have led to a proliferation of ancillary posts for untrained workers. But with rising unemployment and chronic problems of homelessness amongst single people in city areas, most services have also appointed ancillary 'job seekers' and 'housing workers' as well as using volunteers to lead groups in social skills, literacy, and so on.

The effect of all these divisions of labour has been to obscure the changing nature of the job, and the changing fortunes of the clientele. Twenty years ago the vast majority of probation clients were employed, had settled accommodation, and were independent of the social services – with the exception of recidivist ex-prisoners. Nowadays, the vast majority are unemployed, and many more are homeless drifters. By taking on ancillaries to concentrate on the material and practical problems of offenders, the trained probation staff can continue to work in much the same way as before, concentrating on office interviews, investigating motivations, attitudes to authority, family patterns and emotional reactions, as if nothing has changed.

The organizational fragmentation of the personal services, and the division of labour within them, helps to obscure the structural origins of clients' problems. The essence of traditional social work is finding solutions to individual problems – an approach which fits well into the liberal democratic individualist tradition of the British political system. By breaking down social work's tasks into small pieces, as well as dividing up communities into individual 'cases', the overall picture is lost. Each bit *seems* to make sense. An ancillary helps an unemployment man to improve his interview skills. An advice centre tells him of his welfare rights. The probation officer counsels him on attitudes to employers. None of them address themselves to the fact that there are 15 other similar people, with similar problems, applying for every job, or waiting at every understaffed social security office.

In the same way, some policies which make good humane sense for individuals make a different sort of sense in aggregate. The strong development of a movement in the field of child care (The British Agencies for Adoption and Fostering) which campaigns for permanent substitute homes (ideally adoption) for all children who stay in care for more than six months, is clearly in the interests of individual children of a certain age who have lost their links with natural parents. But in a society where many parents cannot care for their children because of material deprivation and the lack of the essentials for a decent and secure life, such a *policy* will eventually lead to more and more children being taken from poor families (especially single parents) and placed in better-off families (especially middle-class ones). No wonder single parent organizations lobby against the permanence movement, and advise their members to avoid social workers. The situation is reminiscent of the strong trend in the USA for children to be statutorily removed from black families, and placed with white parents for adoption – a trend which was not altered until black social workers refused to implement the policy any further.

Social workers can identify changes in the drift of policy, as well as explicit changes in legislation and administration. They can monitor the effects of cuts in resources or alterations in priorities. They can campaign on behalf of clients; they can organize and assist groups of clients; they can make alliances with client organizations; they can work through their own trade unions; they can lobby or join political parties. But ultimately they depend on wider changes in political consciousness to alter the nature of their work or the prospects of their clients. For, as Attlee pointed out, the social worker can and should be 'an agitator if he or she learns social facts and believes they are due to certain causes beyond the control of the individual to remove.'[14] Agitation is not just a matter of protests and marches. It is a question of understanding the system of which one is part, helping people affected by its policies to understand it, and adapting and organizing in ways which help bring about change.

Social workers occupy a politically sensitive and significant position in modern societies. As representatives of the state's authority, they have to implemetn laws and policies in relation to groups of people whose lives are being transformed by economic change. The services they administer represent the state's attempt to re-order a society which was once shaped by people's economic roles. Instead of 'communities' of unskilled, low-wage workers and their families, social workers now face 'communities' of unemployment people, single parents and other dependants on state benefits, who have lost their economic positions, and for whom no other social value or significance has been discovered. The notion that these people can be encouraged or organized to form themselves into cohesive and mutually supportive networks is still a vague and pious hope. Meanwhile, social workers are expected (by those who hold political power) to enforce laws whose main emphasis is on damping down social tensions and keeping order.

Yet social workers do not simply represent state power as it confronts these underprivileged groups. If they are imaginatively organized, social work agencies can become forums for a genuine dialogue between deprived people and the state. Social workers can encourage people to identify local issues and needs, and to look for ways of overcoming neighbourhood problems, in partnership with such state agencies as housing departments, schools and the health service. Social workers may be in a specially good position to mediate between groups whose voice is seldom heard in local or national politics, and the powerful state agencies which are constantly dealing with them, but seldom consult them.

In a recent book, Brian Sabel, a local authority social worker, has described his attempts to fulfil just this role in one inner-city area.[15] Active in local Labour Party politics before becoming a social worker, he was struck by the enormous gap between local politicians (even those of working-class origins) and the residents of deprived neighbourhoods. His work has involved encouraging officials and professionals in schools, housing projects, community centres and his own department to meet with groups of residents, tenants and parents to talk about issues, plan for the future, and set up new kinds of provision. The idea sounds simple enough, but it is precisely this kind of partnership between the people and the state's agencies that failed to come about through the growth of these agencies in the 1960s and early 1970s, and which provoked a backlash against the welfare state. Brian Sabel's account provides encouraging evidence that there are opportunities for co-operation and progress, even in the present unfavourable economic climate.

The fact is that even Marxist theory requires that some change should take place in the relationship between the state and its citizens, in line with these recent economic developments. According to Marx, there is a constantly changing relationship between *productive forces* (the resources used in production), *productive relations* (the way in whch capital and labour are combined in production), and the *superstructure* of the state. In our present situation, the development of modern technology and its application to industry have led to what Marx would have called a *contradiction* in the system as a whole. Mass unemployment is a symptom of that contradiction, because it has resulted from a change which caused productive forces to develop in ways which were inconsistent with previous productive relations. This requires the state to adapt itself, and to try to reconcile the contradiction, in whatever way it can.

Most Marxists would argue that under capitalism the state tends to reflect the needs of capitalists (to ensure high levels of profit, and the continued growth of productive forces), and to reflect the class struggle (with capitalists retaining power in ways which can only be modified to some extent by the organized labour movement). But there has been increasing interest in recent years in the idea that the state's institutions, and particularly the social services, might be an arena in which important changes and gains could be made. As the industrial sector shrinks, and the state sector expands, so attention focuses on the public services. Both capital and labour must devote more energy to transforming the state in their interests; but there are also the interests of the 'surplus population', previously excluded from political power, to be considered.

Under a Conservative Government, policy will probably contain a mixture of 'strong' government, with an emphasis on discipline and law and order, and an attempt to rebuild a sense of the 'traditional community'. But for those who, like myself, believe that change will eventually have to be more fundamental, this formula seems to involve more and more control and suppression of discontent. Yet I cannot believe that a Labour Government could ever remove the contradiction between productive forces and productive relations simply by increased government spending and economic planning. The only long-term alternative seems to lie in the emergence of a political movement amongst the dispossessed 'surplus population' itself, and an answering movement amongst organized labour, whose meeting point will be the public services. This would bring about a *political* transformation of the social services, to which social workers could certainly contribute, but which they could not bring about by themselves.

There are some signs of the beginnings of an awareness of the need for such a transformation, in the labour movement, in social work, and to some extent among the dispossessed themselves. How social work might contribute to these changes will be discussed more fully in the final chapter.

REFERENCES

1 Bill Jordan, *Mass Unemployment and the Future of Britain*, Blackwell, 1982, chs 6–8
2 Joan Higgins, *States of Welfare*, pp. 150–58
3 Bill Jordan, *Automatic Poverty*, Routledge & Kegan Paul, 1980, ch. 7
4 See for instance C. Brewer and J. Lait, *Can Social Work Survive?*, Temple Smith, 1980
5 Barclay Committee, *Social Workers, Their Role and Tasks*, Bedford Square Press, 1982
6 *Ibid.*, pp. 257–8
7 M. Cooper, 'Community social work', in Bill Jordan and Nigel Parton (eds), *The Political Dimensions of Social Work*, Blackwell, 1983
8 Barclay Committee, *Social Workers*, p. 220
9 *Ibid.*, p. 222
10 *Ibid.*, p. 224
11 *Ibid.*, pp. 227–8
12 *Ibid.*, pp. 238–9
13 F. Lafitte, 'The relief function', in M. Brown (ed.), *Social Issues and the Soical Services*, Knight, 1974, p. 231
14 Attlee, *The Social Worker*
15 Brian Sabel, 'Community and social services', in Bill Jordan and Nigel Parton (eds), *The Political Dimensions of Social Work*

PART IV
Conclusions

8

Social Work in Action

So far in this book I have introduced what I consider to be the main themes in social work thought and debate – ideas which have influenced the planning, organization and policies of social work. In this chapter I want to try to illustrate how these ideas work out in practice.

This is in some ways the most difficult thing to do, because relatively few social workers describe their practice in much detail; yet it is precisely at the detailed, face-to-face level that the issues I have identified – the moral, social and political dilemmas of social work - are either somehow resolved, or else fudged, evaded or suppressed.

Hence I shall have to rely to a considerable extent on my own experiences, in 20 years of various kinds of social work, to illustrate some of the points to be made. But I shall also draw on others' detailed descriptions (published and unpublished) of their struggles with similar problems.

THE MORAL DIMENSION

In chapters 2 and 3 I tried to show that Victorian social workers saw their work primarily in moral terms, but that this basis for practice decayed in the inter-war years, and was largely replaced in the 1940s and 1950s by psychological theories. I also tried to show that these latter ideas have clear weaknesses as a basis for practice, and have been substantially discredited. Moral dilemmas, which occur daily in social work practice (if the social worker allows himself to be aware of them) stubbornly refuse to be reduced to psychological questions. They remain issues of right and wrong, which cannot be translated into the language of 'needs' or 'drives'.

Recently a student on the course I teach introduced a seminar by describing the kind of situation he had faced many times as a residential social worker, employed in a probation hostel for adult offenders. The residents were mainly people who had become homeless, rootless or isolated, often because of repeated failures in domestic and social relationships. Many of them frequently got drunk, or violent, or stole, or broke the rules of the hostel – behaviour which the staff understood to be 'testing out' the limits of their acceptability, as provoking rejection, as self-destructive or compulsive. Staff would try to tolerate such behaviour for a time, to find constructive ways of dealing with it, but ultimately they would look for punitive solutions, or threats of eviction from the hostel – either asking the liaison probation officer to remove the resident, or to take him back to court, or to recommend imprisonment for a fresh offence.

The student pointed out that it was always possible to rationalize the recourse to punitive measures or rejection. He could tell himself that the resident 'must learn the socially acceptable limits to his behaviour'; 'must learn to recognize reality'; 'must see authority as firm as well as caring'; 'must discover his own motivation for change'; 'needs a more structured environment', and so on. But ultimately he always had a sense of bad faith about such rationalizations. He was conscious that these were exactly the same things (or more pompous versions of the same things) that parents, teachers, employers, wives, neighbours, magistrates and officials had said previously about these clients. If he and his colleagues were simply coming to the same conclusions, repeating the same patterns – perhaps after a slightly longer period of tolerance and forbearance – then wherein lay his claim, as a social worker, to a special ethic of caring and helping, or a special commitment to the needs of these difficult and demanding people?

His value system as a social worker – indeed, his reason for becoming a social worker – consisted in notions about every individual being worthy of respect and help, and everyone (clients and non-clients) as needing help from fellow human beings. This ethical requirement applied irrespective of any psychological explanation of the residents' behaviour. While the notion of unconscious, irrational or self-destructive motivation might strengthen the argument for respecting and caring for an individual, in spite of his actions, the original requirement was logically prior to any such explanations of behaviour. All of us – including social workers – act from a mixture of conscious and unconscious motives, rational and irrational impulses, so the requirement to respect and help others cannot be dependent on the perception of psychological disturbances. The student was conscious that, although he would explain away his punitive feelings and the cold-blooded recommendations for eviction or imprisonment to which they gave rise, they were in fact breaches of the moral code on which his professional identity was based.

This is a good example of how the ethical dimension in social work arises in practice – in feelings (often vague, background, niggling feelings) of uneasiness and self-reproach, feelings which persist in spite of our forthright declarations that we 'had no option' or that 'there was no other choice'; in spite of our colleagues' reassurances that we 'can only do so much', or that 'in the last resort it's up to people to help themselves'; in spite of our superiors' authoritative pronouncements that we were only 'following agency policy', and that to have done otherwise would have been to invite departmental censure. It is the mark of a 'burnt-out' social worker that he no longer ever hears, recognizes or attends to the still small voice of conscience that his less cynical and hardened colleagues frequently get inside their heads, questioning their good intentions or good faith. It is only by attending to such feelings of regret or self-reproach that we can subject our work to any sort of active moral scrutiny.

However, the notion of a constant internal debate over ethical issues is not at all what I am recommending. While it is something like conscience that alerts social workers to moral issues, there is little constructive purpose to be served in their retreating with such issues into a private world of ethical philosophizing. Unfortunately, such is exactly the sort of behaviour which appears to be recommended by the notion of a professional 'code of ethics' – as if the social worker could go home each evening and check over his actions for the day in a private moral manual. In the first place, it is of the essence of any code, personal or professional, that a number of different ethical goals and principles are stated, but that these are often in conflict with each other in real-life situations. Thus choices between principles are often necessary, and there is seldom one 'right' choice which meets every moral requirement equally well. Secondly, the individual is unlikely to be in full enough possession of all the facts about a situation to reach a sound judgement without discussing the basis of his decision with others concerned. This is why a true dialogue on moral issues, rather than an internal struggle with oneself, is likely to lead to better results. Thirdly, if the social worker simply retreats into his moral study, and appears with a decision, this is a form of moral imperialism – imposing his morality on clients in particular, but also on anyone else involved with them. Clients can only learn moral lessons – assuming there are lessons to be learnt – by discussion which calls upon them to evaluate their actions and decisions, and to share in a moral debate. This allows social workers to learn moral lessons too.

What is particularly uncomfortable about the sort of situation which the student described is the feeling by the social worker that he and his colleagues are being driven into making a unilateral decision, to override the resident's long-term interests, and some of his needs and feelings, without any proper discussion of the moral issues involved. Indeed, often the discomfort arises directly from the apparently compulsive inability of the resident to perceive and observe rules which the social worker regards as moral rules (consideration for other residents, honesty, sobriety, etc.), and hence the apparent fruitlessness of any moral discussion. Thus the social worker *seems* to be the only party to the whole transaction who is concerned by moral issues, or plagued by moral scruples – a situation which causes him to feel an unpleasant mixture of guilt and resentment. This in turn makes it difficult for him to share his feeling, or the real issues, with the resident.

Yet it is only through sharing these feelings and issues that a proper resolution of the situation can be sought. In the absence of this sharing, a unilateral solution will be imposed, and the social worker will be left with his guilt, and a sense of unfinished business. Often it is only when he can find a way of telling the resident (or client) of the discomfort he is feeling – including his 'bad' feelings of anger, guilt or fear – that some progress can be made. Once he manages to break out of his own private internal struggle and debate, and open up a real discussion with the resident (or client), he may find that the latter can in turn share quite other feelings than those indicated by his behaviour, and may even confide moral dilemmas of his own. Indeed, a true moral dialogue may then be able to take place, restoring the proper ethical quality of status between worker and client.

Here are a couple of examples of the sort of process I trying to describe. They both concern fieldwork rather than residential work, but they illustrate the same principles. In their book *Mate and Stalemate*, Janet Mattinson and Ian Sinclair described a research project working in a city social services department with hard-core, long-term families, who consumed disproportionate amounts of social work time, and were assessed as having marital problems. The project workers offered regular interviews, focused on the marital relationship; but they also took responsibility for the bewildering multiple demands the families made upon the agency. One project worker became involved in a crisis in the office with Mrs Yates (not a project case), a lady with a grievance against the housing department, whom he first encountered screaming at social workers in their reception area, and smashing furniture. The following was a case record:

'This was not the end of the incident. Later in the afternoon Mrs Yates returned and demanded money for the weekend. It had been decided that no supplementation of her social security money would be made on this occasion, although it had been in the past. It was known she spent large sums of money on long-distance telephone calls and this was why she could not make ends meet.

Mrs Yates did not like our refusal and so demanded that we took the two children into care. However, at the same time she became hysterical about what it would mean to them and insisted that any place they might be taken would be terrible and that they would be ill-treated. She made it impossible for the request to be proceeded with and, while demanding that we took the children from her, clung to them tightly and they to her, so that in order to remove them we would have had to fight her. We refused to do this and insisted that she either hand them over calmly or take them away with her. By this time they were thoroughly distressed, pleading with her to take them away, but she was quite deaf to their pleas.

There then followed a long argument, with her alternately demanding money to see her through the weekend or that we take the children from her. The area officer and I needed each other for support to withstand the fury and obstinacy with which we were confronted. In desperation I asked Mrs Yates why she had to make us behave like such bastards towards her. She screamed that we were bastards and rather wearily I agreed that maybe we were. Almost at once she began to soften and decided to leave with the children. She left us drained and shattered.'

The workers spent an anxious weekend. They wondered whether they had done right and they were concerned lest the children had been put at risk. A further offer of permanent housing came through a week later and, to the workers' surprise, was accepted by Mrs Yates without question.[1]

In another case, the project worker called to make an offer of regular appointments with a couple:

After a number of calls which entailed much fruitless knocking, some discussions with Mr and Mrs Mothersill over the milk bottles on the doorstep, and a half-veiled threat from Mr Mothersill, I was finally allowed into their dark basement flat. The first impression was of enormous clutter, but surprisingly the place contained only one chair. I sat down on this and said I had come to discuss whether they would like me to come once a week to talk over their marital problems. . . . In response they began to shout at each other at the tops of their voices. I could not understand what they were shouting about, so I repeated my question. They continued to shout, and again I repeated my question, and again they went on shouting, the noise they were making getting, if anything, even louder. Eventually I shouted above the din that what they seemed to be asking me was whether I could *stand* coming once a week to discuss their marital problems. At once they fell quiet, and Mr Mothersill then said 'in a manner of speaking' that seemed to be what they were asking.[2]

These are both good examples of social workers managing to communicate with their clients about the essentials of very difficult situations, and doing so under great personal pressure. They also show that moral courage is required to achieve this communication. The social workers both took a risk in saying what they did – a risk of being ridiculed or abused, not merely in their roles (this was happening already in both cases) – but as people. They were saying something about the discomfort they felt, as individuals, in that role, and putting the whole situation (of conflict between people in roles) into a more human context. There is always a sense in which this feels risky and difficult to do, and invites a particularly nasty form of personal rejection and scorn. Yet in both these instances it seemed to enable a far more fruitful dialogue to take place, and to do so almost immediately.

It may be useful if I give an example from my own experience of when I tried to do this, and it appeared to fail dismally. George was a man in his late forties who had had psychiatric treatment since the age of twenty. He had had a serious schizophrenic breakdown soon after starting work in a manual trade and – in the manner of the crude psychiatry of that era – had been given a leucotomy as his treatment. The result was that George, who subsequently grew into a massively strong, intimidating-looking person, developed in a very unpredictable way. During one four-year spell of comparative stability, he held a job, married and produced two children. But soon after that he began a pattern of heavy drinking, stealing and other minor offences, which seemed clearly linked with hallucinations and persecutory anxiety. George could be very violent when he felt under threat, and had assaulted groups of policemen and prison officers who attempted to restrain him. But in his family he was gentle, nervous and retiring.

I had known George for nearly 20 years when this incident occurred – partly as a probation officer, and partly as a psychiatric social worker. His marriage had finally broken up, after George had spent several long spells in psychiatric hospital and in residential care; but his wife had insisted that George should have the chance of living in the family's council house as his home when she eventually remarried, if he chose to do so, sacrificing a very comfortable dwelling, and going to live with the children in a flat. George was keen to take this opportunity, was grateful for his wife's generous gesture, and for a time did well in looking after himself, with quite a lot of support from myself. Unfortunately after a while I had to go abroad for a month, and George began to deteriorate, becoming extremely suspicious, fearful and strange.

One evening, after I had been told of a series of bizarre incidents concerning George, I went to see him on one of my regular visits. He looked tense and frightened, but I had many years of trust between us to rely on. Perhaps I was rather tired or careless, but at some point in our conversation he said something odd about a neighbour, and I foolishly remarked 'Come off it, George.' At this his eyes blazed, his muscles tensed, his fists clenched, he picked up a pair of scissors and shouted 'Don't you tell me to come off it, Bill!' For the first time in all those years I felt afraid of George, I noticed his huge bulk and menacing expression. I was entirely unprepared for this fear. I felt the ground slip from under my feet. In the absence of the trust that I had come to take for granted, I felt I had nothing to offer him. The situation was not helped when the phone rang, and his ex-wife wanted to speak to me. The telephone was right by George's chair, and he did not move. The flex was short, and I found myself in the absurd situation of talking to his ex-wife about George some 18 inches from his nose. She too had had a frightening experience with him (like myself, it was the first time she had been afraid) and wanted to communicate her concern. But this merely reinforced my own anxiety. After I had spoken to her, I found it hard to think of anything but getting out of the house, more and more conscious of George's long scissors, and the knife near his other hand. I feebly withdrew, mumbling empty phrases.

No sooner had I driven away than I felt a powerful sense of self-disgust. Because I was afraid I had simply fled, severing George's last links with a source of support, help and treatment. George had not trusted me, and I had shown myself unworthy of trust – I had let him down. Worst of all, I had failed to show him that I understood his fear, and had been afraid myself. I called to see a friend of mine who lived nearby, and who had visited George while I was abroad. I kicked myself all round his front room, upbraiding myself for my cowardice and lack of social work principle. Eventually I came to a decision – it was no good, I had to go back.

I knocked on George's door, but he came to the nearby window. He didn't open it, but asked me what I wanted. It was dark and the street was deserted, but I felt self-conscious as I asked to be allowed back in, as I had something more I wanted to say. George told me I could say it through the window, though he made no move to open it. I said I would much prefer to come in to say it. He insisted that I remain outside. I asked him at least to open the window. He told me brusquely to hurry up and get it said. I glanced up and down the street, aware that I was making a complete fool of myself – fortunately there was no one about, though I was sure the neighbours were listening as I was forced to speak very loudly to let George hear. I took a deep breath, and reminded George of all the years we had known each other, and some of the more alarming incidents that had taken place. I said I realized that George must be very frightened at present, because that evening, when he reacted so sharply, I had been frightened, and I had never felt this with him before. When I had said this, George commented, 'Fair enough', sat down and went on watching television. I was left outside, very conscious that an unbiased observer would probably conclude that I, not George, was out of my mind. But I went home feeling rather less displeased with myself than before.

Although George appeared to have ignored my attempt to communicate with him about the whole situation, subsequent events suggested that something of what I was trying to say had got through to him. I arranged for an ex-patient friend of his to visit regularly – the only person he would receive in the house – and although there was much anxiety about George by all concerned, and all the relevant authorities were notified, nothing drastic occurred. Eventually, one weekend George became convinced that the IRA had bombed his house, walked three miles to his mother's home in his bedroom slippers, and asked her to telephone me. Having been adamant that he did not want to go to hospital, George now readily accepted my offer to take him there, and indicated that his trust in me had been at least partly restored. Eventually George arranged his own return to residential care.

All these examples are of extreme situations, in which social workers often feel both that moral dilemmas are most acute, and that moral dialogue is least possible. In fact I suspect that even people in very acute emotional distress – including madness – retain a moral sense, and can recognize courage and commitment. This is why brave and caring residential social workers are so seldom injured, even though they deal with people who are dangerous in other situations, and why the physically weak but morally courageous are often most successful in dealing with alarmingly violent situations.

When my colleague Jean Packman and myself were collecting material for an article on training social workers for working with violence, several of our women ex-students gave us examples of where they had intervened in violent situations, with apparently rash disregard for their safety, and had not been injured. Some of these were instinctive reactions to violence. In one case a young woman probation officer visited a couple the same day as the husband had threatened to kill his wife. During the interview, the man became very angry and started to hit his wife. The probation officer at once grabbed his arm and told him to stop it. He did so, and there was no further violence. In another example a young woman, who was then an unqualified social work trainee, was called to the scene of a siege, by policemen and Alsatian dogs, of a house where a man with a shotgun was barricaded with his wife and children. The man had originally threatened an official of the Electricity Board who had come to disconnect their supply. The social worker asked the police to withdraw (which they did under protest), gained access to the house simply by walking up to the door, and found that the man was (after initial suspicion) very willing to talk to her. She was able eventually to negotiate a settlement with the Electricity Board.[3]

The social workers in these examples were risking injury or even death because they were in no position to enforce any kind of physical submission on the participants. The success of their interventions seemed to depend to a great extent on the perception of this fact by the violent person, and the recognition of their actions as expressions of true concern and willingness to help. I myself have experienced a situation in which someone I stopped from hitting his wife actually drew back his fist to hit me, and then stopped fighting altogether. It is difficult to specify the cues by which very angry (or even apparently uncontrollably drunk) people pick up this quality in the actions of social workers, but these and other incidents suggest that some such process occurs in violent and other stressful encounters. It may well be that some such perception of the moral quality of social work interventions has been an important and neglected aspect of the potential influence and effectiveness of social work.

THE SOCIAL DIMENSION

The second dimension of social work was discussed in chapters 4 and 5. In these chapters I argued that the employment of social workers in state agencies endowed these workers with roles and functions which were quite different from the ones taken by their voluntary charitable predecessors. These new roles, as part of the official machinery of state systems of welfare, justice and control, gave new dilemmas as well as new opportunities.

The sense of 'social' that was chiefly discussed in those chapters was the same sense as is implied in the general term 'social services', i.e. organized provision, including state services, using collectivized resources, and in pursuit of a policy objective. Once such services are established, workers within them tend to take their existence for granted, even though they continue to argue about methods, objectives, priorities, and so on. Some contemporary issues of this nature were discussed in these earlier chapters.

Yet there is also a sense in which the notion of 'social' in social work has slightly different connotations from this very general sense of the word. For instance, the health service, education, housing and social security are all *social* services in this broad, general sense; but the notion of 'social' in *social work* implies something rather distinct. Indeed, it implies an approach that is distinguishable precisely in that it is *non*-medical, *non*-educational, and concerned with something other than the bureaucratic provision of money or accommodation. What exactly this different approach actually entails, and how social workers can justify it to colleagues and critics in the other services, is often a day-to-day struggle for social workers to define and defend.

This sense of the word 'social' is concerned with people's lives together in families, groups, neighbourhoods, communities and societies – their attitudes, behaviour, expectations, norms, influences, organizations and aspirations. It tends to analyse all these aspects of human needs and problems in terms of environment and social interaction. It emphasizes that apparently 'abnormal' or 'deviant' actions often make sense and can be understood in their social contexts. This understanding owes something to politics and economics as well as to sociology and social psychology.

The kind of approach that social workers have developed has been less scientific and precise than those of others professions, but more flexible and informal. The clearest contrast is with medicine. Doctors are trained in a scientific way, and encouraged to think of themselves as applied scientists, making their diagnoses and prescribing treatments according to carefully considered evidence. In order to gain this evidence, to make scientific assessments, the patient is examined under clinical conditions or samples of tissues are sent to laboratories. If the condition is serious, he is removed to hospital for tests. Diagnosis and treatment are therefore carried out under scientific auspices, and mainly outside the patient's social context. In fact, many medical judgements contain important moral, social and political elements, as Ian Kennedy showed in his 1980 Reith Lectures. But doctors are encouraged to play down these elements, to deny their implications, and to concentrate on the professional and clinical aspects of their work, subsuming all the other aspects under the dominant guise of objective, neutral, applied scientist.

As a result of this professional persona, doctors have gained much power, status and prestige. But the role of professional scientist has entailed developments in medicine which are now at last coming under criticism. Medical services have clustered around hospitals, where expensive technologies for rare illnesses have mushroomed. But deprived communities have been neglected, and primary health care has been far less generously resourced. Preventive aspects of medicine are now recognized as more vital influences on rates for the most widespread illnesses than curative treatment, yet the medical profession has seldom taken a lead in these matters, or encouraged resources to be diverted to them. Many of the greatest contributions to public health – for instance, in ensuring clean water supplies – have been pioneered by non-medical people, in the face of indifference from doctors.

Furthermore, while insisting on their scientific probity, doctors have usually practised according to the moral assumptions of their time. For instance, in the late nineteenth century, attitudes to mentally subnormal people were dominated by the notion that they were a threat to society. They were seen essentially 'as manifestations of the lower nature of civilised man, barely kept under control by the forces of society.'[4] Hence provision for the mentally subnormal in 'asylums', under medical supervision, gave highest priority to the protection of society, by putting such people in isolated institutions, and enforcing a deadening routine, calculated to control their potentially violent, animal-like, primitive natures. Doctors must take a very large share of the moral responsibility for the fact that they have continued to this day to play the most powerful roles in such a system of 'care' and 'treatment', which owes little to true science.

We saw in chapter 4 that social work was incorporated into the state's social provision as a way of ridding our services of the legacy of the Poor Law. But this legacy was also in part the responsibility of the older professions, all of which had played some part in the callous treatment given to the most vulnerable members of our society in the pre-war era. In creating the post-war personal social services, the political architects of the welfare state were trying to create a new kind of service, staffed by people with a new approach to provision for those traditionally stigmatized, degraded or neglected groups.

In many ways social work has succeeded in developing such an approach. It has been an influence towards humanizing harsh institutions; towards community care; towards the 'normalization' of behaviour previously seen as intolerable; towards informal negotiation with people, rather than legal compulsion or 'doctors' orders'. But this was not something that could be achieved at a single stroke, nor is the battle ever over. Social workers constantly struggle against strong pressures within society towards perceiving and treating clients in the old ways. There are also forces within social work itself that would like to change it into a different sort of profession, to make it more like medicine, education, or the law.

In day-to-day practice, social workers are constantly in touch with doctors, schools and lawyers, as well as with officials of the other state services. They are able to exert some influence on these other professions, but they are very open to pressure from them. Part of the trouble stems from the fact that the social services department is seen as a dustbin agency where other services can send their rejects – those they perceive as too feckless, too deviant, too confused, too demanding, too difficult to make proper use of what is on offer in the way of treatment, education or benefits. Hence the notion of 'social' in social work becomes a derogatory label, rather than a distinctive approach. When a doctor says that something is a 'social problem, not a medical one' he is often making a disguised value judgement about his patient, implying that he or she is part of the vague and disliked category of 'welfare cases' whose needs can best be left to social workers.

I am particularly aware of the dangers of this kind of process in my dealings with schools. It has been recognized for some time that certain schools 'manufacture' delinquents and deviants in much larger numbers than others do. Research has shown that once teachers perceive pupils as having difficult home backgrounds or 'social problems' they treat them differently, and that this influences how they are assessed at school, and ultimately how they perform – even if the information on which the original judgement was made was inaccurate. Conversely, if pupils are seen as coming from 'good homes' they are more favourably assessed, even if they in fact have severe difficulties at home.[5] Generally teachers know very little about children's home lives, and make such judgements from slender evidence. Even more important than classroom teachers are form tutors, heads of year, assistant heads and so on; they are in a powerful position to influence the pupil's school identity. Schools which have developed systems of 'pastoral care' based on these roles reduce the influence of classroom teachers, especially in relation to outside agencies, which have to deal directly with pastoral care staff. I have found that certain schools which have developed this system identify a group of children as 'troublemakers' at a fairly early stage in their secondary education; and from that point onwards the process is largely one of self-fulfilling prophecy.

At some stage in their school careers, children who are perceived as difficult by such schools may be referred to social workers as 'beyond their parents' control' or 'in need of care'. The notion of such children as having 'social problems' becomes synonymous with the idea that they are beyond the pale of the school, and should be removed – not only from the school itself, but also from their homes and neighbourhoods. In my experience, pastoral staff can put very strong pressure on social workers to take the drastic step of applying for a care order, without ever properly considering the implications of this for the child or the parents. 'Care' becomes a convenient disposal for children who do not happen to fit into that particular school system, and a 'social problem' comes to mean anyone who defies the authority or expectations of key staff. The importance of schools in the processes by which children come into care is shown by the fact that more children are committed under the section of the 1969 Children and Young Persons Act dealing with the lack of 'an efficient full-time education' than for parental cruelty or neglect.

I would argue that the 'social approach' offered by social workers should not represent a means of such children being rejected by mainstream education, but a way of reintegrating them into it, wherever possible. In particular, social workers tend to be more aware of the damaging effects on a child's development and identity of coercive removal from home and school, of an institutional placement, and of isolation from friends and social activities. But this approach often has to be fought for in the teeth of vehement opposition from other major agencies.

Take the case of Michael, who is nearly fifteen. I have known him for some two and half years, and throughout this time the pastoral care staff of his school have been complaining that he is unacceptable to them. At first he wasn't going to school, and they threatened court action over that; then, when he attended school much more regularly, his behaviour was described as disruptive. Eventually Michael was expelled, for spitting on the door-handle of his head of year. At about the same time, he was reported by the police for a series of offences of theft; most of the property was recovered. The most serious theft was from the school. The police are equally adamant that Michael is a real villain, and should have been 'put away' long ago – even though these are his first offences. They say that he needs 'discipline' that can only be taught him in a detention centre or a community school.

Why is Michael so disliked by teachers and police? His behaviour at school was probably no worse than that of a dozen other boys in his year, and there are many others of his age with a much worse criminal record. The answer may well lie in a combination of his family circumstances and his appearance. Michael's elder brother was very unpopular with the school, and got into some minor trouble with the police – he has now left school and got a job, and his critics have forgotten him. His parents are known to have health problems. Michael himself is well-built and good-looking, but has an irritable, defiant facial expression. He is in fact a rather timid lad, who reacts very defensively to criticism. Disliked from the start of his schooldays by certain staff, he has developed a surly and rebellious *look* about him, that provokes still further attention. The whole process has become circular.

Michael's parents find him difficult to handle. At times he has been incredibly rude and provocative; at others he flies into uncontrollable rages. There have been moments when they have despaired of being able to manage him. But on balance they believe that he will grow up to be a hard-working and capable young man, with many good qualities, able to be kind and considerate, independent and adventurous. They find the attitude of the school and police towards him upsetting, and want to keep him in the family if at all possible.

Since Michael has been expelled, he has had a home tutor, provided by the education authority. The tutor likes Michael, and takes him shooting. He does not share the opinions of the school or the police. He finds Michael willing and co-operative. He will come to court when Michael appears, and speak for him.

I have to write a report for the court. It is my job as a social worker to put Michael's behaviour into its whole social context. I shall not attempt to disguise the bad opinions there are of Michael by the school and the police. But I shall also make sure that the court is aware of his good qualities and his parents' commitment to his future success. They may also remember his brother, and be encouraged by the fact that he has grown through his troublesome period. Finally I shall point out that before a care order can be made, every other alternative should be tried. In spite of his unpopularity, Michael is at a very early stage of delinquency. I shall recommend a supervision order, and hope that I can continue to work with Michael and his parents, as I have been previously on a voluntary basis. My aim is to be able to see Michael through a difficult stage in his life, with confidence that he will emerge from it quite a good citizen, if nothing too drastic is done to him.

I have described the 'social' element in social work as sharply distinguished from the therapeutic, pedagogic or legal approaches of the 'ancient professions'. But real dilemmas arise because, while the 'social' element is the ingredient that makes social work different and potentially special, it cannot be separated off from these other aspects. State social work has a legal basis, and the most difficult and complex responsibilities of social workers are defined by statute. While some residential work is concerned with giving humane care alone, much contains elements of 'training', and some of education. Above all, in so far as social work is involved in trying to influence or change people's behaviour, it has links with psychotherapy, and uses similar methods at times. All this means that – quite apart from the close connections between social work and the 'ancient professions', and its dependence on their decisions in many settings – social workers have to incorporate their distinctive social insights and methods into structures which owe much to the older approaches of medicine, law and education.

For instance, most of my present part-time social work job is concerned with a clinic in a medium-sized market town. The clinic is officially part of the psychiatric services, in so far as all the other employees work for the health service, and their experience has mainly been of work in hospitals. There is a psychologist, a psychiatric nurse and an occupational therapist, but no doctor. The clinic was set up, without any very clear policy aims or priorities, to take referrals from general practitioners, psychiatrists and social workers, and to provide a local resource for an area which had previously been served only by the old Victorian psychiatric hospital (15 miles away), a psychiatric day hospital (seven miles away) and a weekly out-patients' clinic by one of the consultant psychiatrists.

In the absence of proper planning and monitoring (which, with its tradition of 'clinical autonomy', the health service notoriously lacks) such an initiative raises as many dilemmas as it provides solutions. Does the clinic canvas for clients, or does it passively wait for referrals? Does it concentrate on a particular group of potential beneficiaries – such as women with anxiety problems – or does it take whatever comes? Does it adopt a particular therapeutic method, and stick to it, or is it eclectic and adaptable according to its clientele? Does it try to respond to urgent cases by prompt action, or does it deal with referrals strictly by date order? Does it use individual therapy or group methods? Does it concentrate its efforts exclusively within the clinic itself, or does it move out into people's homes, and work in their natural settings? Is it primarily concerned with a preventive approach, focusing on early symptoms of distress, or does it provide after-care and support for people with long careers of mental illness, who are trying to re-establish their lives in the community?

In the absence of clearly agreed priorities and objectives, there are no procedures for settling such issues. Unfortunately, the tradition of the health service is that these dilemmas are seldom directly discussed, but decisions are taken by doctors (as the highest-status professional group). These decisions are usually made in the name of clinical efficiency, clinical responsibility, medical ethics and so on, but many more covert social and even political considerations play their part, as well as simple inertia and conservatism. The result tends to be a hierarchical system, with narrowly medical priorities, responsibilities delegated from medical authority, and a great deal of wasted potential.

In our structure, however, since there was no doctor there could be no such traditional solution. But the danger was that the result could be similar. A brief power struggle would take place, after which all the issues mentioned could have been settled, without any of them being properly discussed. Whichever discipline triumphed could have imposed its priorities on the rest of the team, leaving them to make whatever use they could of their particular skills in a system which owed little to their ideals and aspirations. The alternative was for there to be real discussion of priorities, with each of the dilemmas mentioned being aired, and a solution to them sought which represented the best possible pooling of the team's full potential. This approach required continuous review and revision, and the possibility of radical change.

In attempting the latter approach we were, of course, constantly in danger of drifting into the former, and the whole process was at times extremely uncomfortable. In the early stages of the clinic, I found the psychologist's precise skills in assessing individual clients daunting as well as impressive. I felt 'deskilled' in attempting to emulate her approach, and for a while lost confidence in my own contribution to the team's work, in spite of my many years of experience. However, at other times other members of the team felt equally in jeopardy as a result of proposals for change that I made, whether for more group work, for closer links with local social workers, or for more work in clients' homes. This was because for one or more of them each of these suggestions meant entering into unfamiliar territory, where their established skills and methods did not seem adequate to the tasks.

What has eventually evolved in the clinic seems to me to be a good mixture of the therapeutic and the social approaches. The clinic is now held in a community centre – a friendly place, not at all associated with either health or social services. Most people are seen by appointment, but those with doubts or difficulties about attending are visited at home, and home visits are always an option during treatment. When people arrive, they are seen individually at first, and asked to describe the difficulties they are experiencing, and how they would like to change, or their life to improve. Sometimes they are seen by more than one member of the team, over several weeks. Then we draw up a list, classifying the problems they have told us, and check this with them – they keep a copy of it, and another copy is sent to the person who referred them. From that point, they are offered some kind of treatment by one or more of the team, invited to join one of our groups (relaxation, women's group), or referred to some other more appropriate facility.

Over two-thirds of the 120 people referred to us during the first year the clinic has been at its present location have accepted treatment from us – of the rest, some never arrived at all, and many found the assessment process clarified issues for them, and required no further treatment. Only one of those actually treated has required admission to psychiatric hospital during the year, and only two of those seen by us but not treated have been admitted – both of them choosing this course as preferable in their particular circumstances. My research from the psychiatrists' records, shows that a very noticeable impact has been made on the numbers referred to them for out-patient treatment. During the second six months after we opened our clinic the referral rate of new patients to psychiatric out-patient clinics from our catchment area was less than half the rate during the six months before we opened. Also, during the year we have been available, the referral rate of all patients to the day hospital from our catchment area has been less than half the previous year's rate.

What this seems to show is that a fairly low-key, flexible, local facility providing a non-medical approach, and supplementing primary health care teams and other local resources, can largely substitute for specialist psychiatric attention in the first instance. Our referral rate was higher than that to the psychiatric out-patients' clinic in the previous year, which suggests that general practitioners, who refer more than three-quarters of our clients, see us as a preventive service, rather than as a last resort, and refer people earlier, when their problems are less acute. We hope that in the long run this will mean that far fewer people from our area will enter on a 'psychiatric career', involving being labelled 'mentally ill', or being admitted to mental hospital. But so far we have not significantly altered the rate of admissions to psychiatric hospital from our area. This is not surprising. About four-fifths of admissions nationally in any one year are in fact *re-admissions*, i.e. returns to hospital of people previously admitted, who have therefore embarked on a 'psychiatric career', and taken on the identity of a 'mental patient'. Our long-term aim is to reduce the numbers of people who ever enter that process, by substituting a non-medical non-institutional approach to problems of day-to-day life. This will take at least five years to bear fruit, we suspect; and it will also take persistence in showing our more traditional referral agents that our methods really work, and that we can contain and help more demanding and difficult people than they imagine.

But in addition to this objective in what has been a traditionally medical field, we have also succeeded in establishing good links with the local social services office. They seconded one of their social workers to us for a year, and this greatly helped liaison and the development of a 'social approach'. By tradition there has been far less overlap between clinical and social services provision than is logical. Many people referred to local social workers by doctors, schools, police, etc., have been selected on criteria such as social class, poverty, material problems, child care difficulties and so on, and could benefit greatly from the services of our clinic. We have been delighted that a number of referrals of their more difficult clients have been made by local social workers, and we have been able to work in close co-operation with them, often tackling issues of child care together in a rather different and potentially constructive way.

Perhaps it would be useful if I gave an example of a case in which my contribution, as a social worker, seemed distinctive. This occurred when the clinic was in its previous location, in another town. Reg, aged seventy, and frail-looking, was referred to us as depressed and lethargic. At first he could say little about himself or his problems, but with encouragement he revealed that he had been a highly skilled engineer in his working days, and a brilliant if eccentric amateur inventor, a charming man whose council house and garden were stocked with novel devices of his creation. Reg had been seriously ill ten years previously, had had to leave his lifelong occupation, and had become depressed and rather dependent on his forthright, no-nonsense wife May. She was mainly concerned about one problem – Reg had fairly recently committed an offence of shoplifting and had a court appearance, and she was terrified of a recurrence of this.

We worked with Reg and May for a time, and he became

much more cheerful and active, and left the clinic. But one day Reg arrived unexpectedly, and in a terrible state. He was almost mute with distress, weeping and holding his head. It emerged that he had been shoplifting again, that although he had not been prosecuted this had come out, and May was beside herself with fury, threatening never to let him see his grandchildren again. He hinted at suicide, and also at the need to be admitted to hospital; my colleagues were alarmed at his condition, and thought an admission was indicated, but I suggested an alternative course. I walked home with Reg, and we waited until May returned from shopping. She was an distressed as Reg, but it all came out in angry rejection – with Reg mainly, but also with us and the doctor for not listening to her, and for not taking his shoplifting seriously. Reg listened in frozen alarm as she described his intolerable behaviour – his obstinate and rather manic activity up to the offence, his self-destructive depression since – and said that either he must be admitted or she would leave, perhaps to hospital herself. I acknowledged our fault in not listening well enough to her, and her real distress. But I tried to reach the sadness and fear behind her anger, pointing out that they were near the end of their lives, had had a good – if sometimes stormy – marriage, and how Reg, if he went into hospital at this stage, might well die there. Eventually May burst into tears, and went and embraced Reg, so that they were weeping together. I visited again that evening and several times during the week, keeping in touch by telephone between visits. The general practitioner was very supportive and concerned, and a home visit was paid by a psychiatrist. Reg was put on a new medication, and gradually the storm died down. In weeks normality was restored. I kept in touch with them by regular visits until Reg's death, some two years later, and I still see May now. Although his final years were difficult, they were together, and May's memories of him are happy ones.

THE POLITICAL DIMENSION

In chapters 6 and 7, I argued that the place of social work in the welfare state, and as part of social policy, gave social workers inevitable dilemmas about the political dimension of their work. However hard they and others might try to define their work in purely professional terms as politically neutral, day-to-day political debate and conflict draws the opposite lesson. As I am writing this, the press leak of cabinet papers revealing government ministers' thoughts on policy towards the family indicates an attempt to 'remoralize' whole sections of the population, restore Victorian notions of marital roles and personal responsibilties, re-educate adults and children, and reduce expectations of state aid. Social workers would certainly be expected to play a part in any such political realignment of social policy objectives. Yet at a local level, many left-wing authorities are fighting against central government policies and resource constraints. These councils require social workers to play their part in encouraging greater public awareness of social need, and willingness to shoulder financial burdens. The experiences of working in right- or left-wing local authorities are becoming more diverse all the time, as the political component in social service provision becomes more overt.

Thus today's social workers are required to be much more aware of their own political philosophy, and of how it applies to their daily practice. If in the past there was often a vague tension between one's consciousness of political goals and one's choice of social work means, that tension has now become much more acute and pressing; it is also much more part of the agenda of discussions between team members and wider colleague groups, at trade union branch meetings, in conferences and on training courses.

Socialist write have for many years pointed out repressive features of state social work practice, and argued for the development of a 'socialist practice', more consistent with this political philosophy. But the search for a thorough-going congruence between theory and practical action is unrealistic. As Bruce Britton points out:

there is a remarkable naivety in thinking that such consistency is possible in a capitalist society. No other worker is in this fortunate position; indeed it is an indicator of the necessity for change that such inconsistencies exist. However, it is just as naive to contend that, because social workers work under capitalism, their every action is reformist. Obviously, this would condemn any activity within any sector of social life as reformist and would allow for no struggle against capitalism at all.[6]

Even the mundane activities which form the elements of day-to-day social work can be seen to be political in their implications. Everyday encounters between social workers, as representatives of the state, and clients, as representatives of deprived groups and communities, of minorities or 'deviant subcultures', can be recognized as containing negotiations over conflicts of interest. Although power is usually very unevenly distributed in such encounters, issues of authority, legitimacy, the limits to protest, social and civil rights are often all present. Professional skills may be used by social workers to achieve reconciliations – between rival interests, or between the state and an individual or group – but some framework for negotiation, some procedure for putting matters at issue 'on the table', and some implicit or explicit settlement of disputes are necessary in any such process.

The difference between social workers and other state officials is that as negotiators they are usually informal and low-key. The forum for negotiations is usually the interview room at the office or the client's own home. There are often no precise definitions of the client's rights or the state's duties; in many cases there are several vague definitions, and some conflict between them – for instance, the legal responsibility on social workers to help families wherever possible to keep children out of care, but to receive children into care wherever necessary for their proper development. Voluntary agreements are generally preferred as outcomes, rather than statutory orders – though in some of the most politically sensitive and risky areas of work, such as child abuse, or adolescent deviance, some social workers increasingly prefer court decisions and clear legal powers. In general, social workers prefer to offer their clients choices, and to engage their co-operation in achieving outcomes where possible. The notion of 'self-determination' is an aim in social work, if not always one that is accomplished.

These matters are small-scale, and often individual, in their manifestations; but they are important, for each encounter between a social worker and a client contributes to the relationship between the state and its citizens. When these encounters are added up we can see the direction in which policy and practice is tending – sometimes drifting, sometimes being driven by political pressure. When researchers discover that the number of compulsory emergency removals of children from their parents has doubled, trebled or quadrupled since 1974 (and no accurate figure can be given) then we have learnt something about the modern state and its relationship to (mainly poor, single-parent) families, and this in turn teaches us something about our political system.

Social workers have a good deal of autonomy in their dealings with clients, even though there is a legal framework, and they are accountable to elected committees. Unlike social security officers, whose discretionary powers are increasingly limited through regulations, social workers dispensing material resources can interpret situations and slant assessments in reaching their decisions. Clients often have only their desperation and hardship as the basis of their claim for help, and are at the mercy of workers whose judgement may be influenced by conscious or unconscious political perceptions. A right-wing pressure group in Devon was at one time openly campaigning against what it described as 'permissiveness' and 'left-wing bias' among social workers, arguing for a far more restrictive approach to the provision of material assistance to 'irresponsible' clients, and the restoration of 'conventional' standards of morality and personal responsibility. Their spokesman, a divisional director of social services, commented in the local press,

We also feel that social workers should only dispense welfare when they are certain that the person is making every effort to fend for himself. People can ask for more and more money from the state, saying that they cannot cope on what they are given, but those are often the people who have colour television and continue to smoke and drink regularly.[7]

Such attitudes are probably common among social security

officers, and are in many ways embodied in the social security regulations themselves. However, at least the claimant has some protection in the existence of written regulations, and the right of appeal against decisions. The danger of the informality and vagueness of social work negotiations is that often no such rules for settling issues exists, and no such rights of appeal, while tacit or overt judgements, including value judgements and moral assessments, are constantly influencing decisions.

On the other hand, the very vagueness and flexibility of social work can make it a potentially valuable means of settling complex and sensitive issues, involving intimate feelings and close relationships, without recourse to formal tribunals or judicial coercion. At one level this can be seen in such apparently 'non-political' fields as divorce and custody proceedings. New conciliation services have been established (pioneered by a voluntary group in the Bristol area) to help couples who are divorcing settle issues about custody of and access to their children. The aim of the schemes is to invite couples to settle contentious issues through negotiation, and to reach agreed conclusions, rather than to fight each other through their lawyers, and for one party or other to 'win' the judge's decision. The social work approach thus substitutes discussion and voluntary agreement for the traditional adversarial model of court arbitration.

In a similar way, social workers can play an important part in settling disputes between people and other state agencies, or with their own agencies. Issues can be clarified and their implications properly considered, where previously there was misunderstanding and mistrust. The social worker can act as an advocate for the client (as in social security or housing tribunals), or there can be specially arranged meetings between representatives of the agencies and the clients. But case conferences, review meetings and co-ordinating committees can take many forms. They can be either secret cabals of professionals, plotting against the civil liberties of individuals and families; or they can be opportunities for those same individuals and families to air their differences with those professionals, and draw up a contract for future action.

Social workers are in a powerful position, as being often those most closely in touch with the people concerned, to influence the way in which these meetings develop, in one direction or the other.

If clients are excluded, are not kept informed on the real issues, or are told of decisions when it is too late to influence them, then these are all steps in the direction of injustice and repression – a loss of civil and social rights. If clients are prepared for such meetings, made aware of the real questions to be settled, given opportunities to express their views and needs, treated as worth listening to, and included in the real discussion of issues, then real participation has occurred. Participation means that ordinary people can influence events, have choices, and that they are encouraged to take action in their own interests. This is of political significance, even if the occasion is a case conference in a mental hospital, or a review meeting in a children's home. Ultimately a democracy is not participation in the full sense if people are systematically excluded from arenas where such crucial decisions are made about their lives.

If this is true at the individual level, it is even more true at the group and neighbourhood level. One of the most persistent features of 'democracy' in Britain, the USA and the Western European countries is that the poorest and most marginal citizens, who receive most attention from the welfare state, play the least active part in the political process. Writers have repeatedly noted that they vote less than other groups, that they form fewer organized pressure groups, that they achieve less control over decisions taken about their local facilities, that they throw up fewer leaders, and so on. Even programmes which have attempted to increase participation in such areas have, on the whole, failed – partly through the apathy of the deprived groups, partly through resistance from the more established groups and political leaders.

Yet social workers and their departments may have an important part to play in involving such people in activities which further their interests, and engage them in the political process. Brian Sabel (see p. 146), who had become disappointed with attempts to bridge the gap between local polities and the residents of deprived areas through his political party and voluntary groups, writes about his work in a social services department, in which he was able to develop community links with his agency as part of his job. Concentrating on community centres, schools, churches and some voluntary groups, and working patiently with residents while they learnt to identify and express their needs, and to trust him, he describes the progress he has made in five years of this work in one inner-city neighbourhood. He concludes:

First, it has very much confirmed my view that the formal political representatives do not generally manage to focus on and achieve significant change in those shared aspirations of their constituents which are more than individual concerns. This is not always because of lack of individual effort or commitment, but it seems to me more because there is little grounding in or knowledge of how communities work, how to organize them or the level at which change can be achieved. Some of the elected representatives do have a close ear to the views of their constituents, but cannot adequately use that knowledge to achieve effective change. My experience also suggests that if one can activate neighbourhood groups to achieve an involvement in the affairs of the immediate locality, this can lead to an interest and involvement in the political and social needs of the wider area, and by combining with the skills of the professionals in the area, influence policy change at local authority level.[8]

But Brian Sabel warns that even committed 'community' social workers can be tempted to desert their informal, unattached activities with the local population, and be drawn back into the more structured safety of the office and its round of meetings and conferences:

The most exciting, exacting and challenging part of my work has been the direct encouragement of residents' participation. There seems to be always a clear tendency for 'community' workers to limit themselves more and more to contacts with fellow professionals and to thereby distance themselves from local people. I am constantly aware of this pressure, which seems to derive from the comfortable feeling of support and mutual cultural assumptions which fellow professionals share. I find myself having consciously to make myself aware of these feelings so that I do not fall into the trap of spending more and more of my time away from local people and cosily ensconced with fellow professionals. To some extent I find myself in a small minority in my own department, and outside it, in insisting on keeping ordinary day-to-day links with local people. This seems to be the area where social services in particular and professionals in general feel least secure.[9]

Yet this may be, as Brian Sabel suggests, precisely the area where social services departments have the greatest potential to contribute, both to the effectiveness of the 'professional' elements in the welfare state, and to the integration of deprived, minority and 'deviant' groups into the political life of our society. Indeed, if social workers cannot get closer to the people of their areas in the ways he describes, and tune in better to their needs, then the only long-term prospect may be for them to become more and more closely identified – both in their official duties and in the public mind – with coercive, non-participatory methods of social control and repression, first of individuals, and later of whole groups and neighbourhoods.

For there is a real danger in our society of a far wider margin of disaffected, alienated citizens, discarded by the economic system, outsiders in the political debate, culturally and socially deprived, and left to the mercies of state officials, operating on behalf of a heartless machine of government. Whether or not this occurs may well depend quite substantially on the efforts of today's workers in the welfare state, not least social workers, who are closely in touch with the most marginalized groups. It is largely through these agencies that relationships between the dominant and deprived members of society are conducted.

The process of keeping such people involved in the political process cannot possibly be conflict-free. If they are going to pursue their interests, they will necessarily make demands, and do so with vigour and with anger. My own past experience of community work suggests that when people are allowed to have a voice, and to exert some direct influence on local political decisions, they quickly develop skills and give expression to their needs in quite sophisticated ways, which take account of the complex nature of the political process.

For instance, over ten years ago I was involved in the

formation of a community association on a large estate which consisted mainly of council housing. A survey had revealed that the estate's residents considered themselves deprived of a number of facilities in relation to the rest of the town, and felt they had little influence on important decisions affecting their lives – for instance, the building of a large new additional area of council housing on the estate, without adequate provision of shops, meeting places, play facilities and so on. A large meeting was called, at which local politicians and officials faced an angry audience of residents. Many harsh words were spoken in the first hour and a half of this meeting, with local people giving vent to their strong feelings of exclusion from the political process, of insensitivity by decision-makers to their opinions and needs, of past wrongs and omissions. But once everyone who wanted to speak had had their say, and the politicians and officials had been seen to listen to their grievances, a constructive spirit quickly entered the proceedings. A further meeting was called, which was equally well attended. Positive proposals were put forward; an action committee was formed to liaise with the council; many of the demands made by residents were incorporated into the plans for the new development (a community centre, an adventure playground and a safe play area for younger children); and the community association that was formed is still active.

However, in the long run the notion of participation cannot be incorporated into a political system whose whole tendency is in the opposite direction – to make certain large groups and communities in society powerless outsiders. Politics reflect economic and social relations, and the political process can neither transcend nor offset the economic developments in a society for more than a short period. The relative decline of the British economy, the re-emergence of mass unemployment, the erosion of the welfare state's universalistic principles, all indicate tendencies which are increasingly reflected in the polarization of the major political parties, and the violent disaffection of certain groups. While it is not yet too late to draw the growing armies of redundant people on decaying housing estates into the political process, that process itself must take some long-term account of their need for economic as well as political participation, and a share in decisions about production and distribution, as well as about public funds and resources.

It is difficult to see how this can be achieved within present institutional structures and productive relations. Without a radical vision of the future direction of change, revealing new opportunities for working–class achievements and advances, any gains in participation, energy and commitment by marginal people must necessarily be local and partial. The future pattern of British politics seems to lie between the emergence of a strong political movement which encapsulates and communicates such a vision; or the emergence of a more ruthless, intrusive and controlling state machine. To judge from past experience, the nature of future social work practice will depend very much on which of these two political roads is taken.

TOWARDS A NEW APPROACH

Yet I have argued at the end of chapter 6 that the possibility of a 'better society' emerging will not depend solely on the outcome of conflicts at the economic level, or even on the fundamental struggle over ownership and control of the means of production. Because of the growing size of the 'surplus population' (the non–employed, whether redundant, disabled or retired), and of the state's social services, it will depend also on the evolution of a new kind of state agency, and a new kind of relationship between the state and its citizens. Instead of being staffed by officials who ration and regulate people according to rules, or bring legal sanctions against them, state agencies will have to become focal points for negotiation, consultation and participation.

Up to now, the state has always been seen (by political theorists as well as by politicians) as the organizing and controlling centre of power, the site of central *authority*, which issues commands to its citizens. Thomas Hobbes justified this on the grounds that the power of the state alone prevented anarchy – the 'war of each against all'. Lenin considered that the Russian Revolution could only succeed by the proletariat seizing the agencies of the state, and using its power to suppress the resistance of the capitalist class. Politicians have always acted as if control of state agencies was the major aim of political activity, and as if this control allowed government to organize society according to its vision and priorities.

But with economic change the state's power has become so extensive and pervasive that this one-way direction of influence has become problematic. Elections every five years may give the public the opportunity to change the Government; they do not give it the opportunity to influence much of what state officials do each day to control and constrain their lives. With all the signs pointing towards a further increase in the power of the state through even greater economic dependence upon it, this issue needs to be directly addressed.

In some ways, social workers are just like other state officials. Their statutory duties often make them act in ways which are experienced by their clients as high-handed, authoritarian and oppressive. But in other ways, they provide clues as to how state agencies might operate differently. They are at times capable of a flexibility and a capacity to encourage participation which raises real hopes of a new sort of relationship between the state and its citizens. They can also, at their best, enable better communications between citizens and officials of other agencies.

They have also pioneered new ways of looking at very long-standing social problems. For instance, social work has unquestionably been drawn into more statutory intervention and court action over child abuse. But it has also developed new methods, such as family centres, where actually or potentially 'abusive' parents can bring their children, can get advice and help over how to manage them, and can share some of the burdens of caring for them with day-care staff. Similarly, although research shows that social workers have, if anything, contributed to the increased use of custodial sentences for juveniles, they have also begun to develop, in 'intermediate treatment', new ways of working with groups of teenagers to help them understand and control their behaviour, and avoid the consequences, in punishment and institutional containment, of further offences. This has included bringing them face to face with magistrates, policemen, and often with their victims.

All this amounts to saying that the best in social work offers glimpses of a form of state agency which might be more concerned to conciliate and mediate between citizens' needs, and to provide opportunities for direct political participation. This would require many other economic and political changes before it could be accomplished, but it is important that a start should be made somewhere in the public services, for any movement which might demand such changes to develop.

Early in the nineteenth century, Jeremy Bentham, who was in many ways the theoretical father of the modern state social services, wrote an obscure and unreadable book called the *Constitutional Code*. Most of this book represented a tediously detailed account of lists of state officials and their functions – presumably hilarious to his contemporaries, but uncannily accurate in its anticipation of today's environmental and health services, and the general structure of the public sector. In the main, the duties and responsibilities of these officials were described in such a way as to make it clear that they would direct and regulate society according to the legal commands of the central authority. But on one page of this book of over a thousand pages there was an exception. Bentham described the 'subjudiciary function' of 'benevolent mediation'. It is a near-perfect anticipation of the modern principle of conciliation between parents, and parents and children, in disputes over divorce, custody and access. The clue is perhaps an insignificant as the hope for change; but if as 'benevolent mediation function' is ever to be adequately incorporated into the state's agencies, social work may well be seen as a primary source of its principles.

Throughout this book I have referred to tensions between the moral, social and political dimensions of social work. In many ways, these tensions reflect the structural role of the social worker in society, and in the welfare state. A fundamental political change which altered the ways in which the state's agencies related to its citizens would not abolish this tension. But it would greatly increase the opportunities for a constructive dialogue between social workers and clients on all these dimensions.

At present, social workers often feel trapped by lonely dilemmas over the moral, social and political implications of the decisions they make about their clients. Clients, in turn, feel frustrated and powerless – they feel on the 'receiving end', but unable to influence or change anything. It is only be structural changes, which alter the spirit of the social services, making them more genuinely open and democratic, that a true dialogue can take place. What we need are social services in which social workers and their clients can share views and influence each other's perceptions of moral, social and political issues.

REFERENCES

1 Janet Mattinson and Ian Sinclair, *Mate and Stalemate: Marital Work in a Social Services Department*, Blackwell, 1979, pp. 138–9
2 *Ibid.*, p. 182
3 Bill Jordan and Jean Packman, 'Training for social work with violent families', in J. P. Martin (ed), *Violence and the Family*, Wiley, 1978, pp. 333–4
4 J. Ryan and F. Thomas, *The Politics of Mental Handicap*, p. 119 p. 119
5 D. Hargreaves, *Social Relations in a Secondary School*, Routledge & Kegan Paul, 1967
6 B. Britton, 'The politics of the possible', in Bill Jordan and Nigel Parton (eds), *The Political Dimensions of Social Work*, Blackwell, 1983, p.132
7 *Express and Echo*, Exeter, 25 February 1980
8 Brian Sabel, 'Community and social services', in Bill Jordan and Nigel Parton *The Political Dimensions of Social Work*, p. 123
9 *Ibid.*, p. 123

Postscript

Why become a social worker? And what is involved in training to be one?

This book has attempted to show that social work is more than just applied benevolence. However, the wish to help others is still a *necessary* condition for being any kind of social worker, if not a sufficient condition. As someone involved in training, I read hundreds of statements each year from applicants, and conduct numbers of interviews with would-be social workers. Nearly all say, in one way or another, that they want to help people, and a major part of what I am doing as an interviewer is trying to assess the genuineness of their motivation. Without this original driving force – demonstrated as much in their attitude to friends and acquaintances as in the good works they have found time to do – they are unlikely to survive the demands of full-time social work, or to be of much use to their clients.

However, I also look for many other qualities in an applicant. These include: the ability to understand and make use of his or her own life experiences, including the painful and upsetting ones; capacity for honest self-doubt and self-criticism; an ability to learn from mistakes; inquisitiveness about other people's lives and life-styles, and evidence of the beginnings of insight into the motivations of 'disturbed' people; a combination of humility and determination in the face of intractable problems; passionate concern about at least some aspects of the suffering or injustice in society; the ability to think critically about his or her experiences of helping others; the beginnings of an understanding about how society works, and how it treats its underdogs; resilience in the face of failure; a sense of humour; and some absorbing interests or ways of relaxing outside work. No one would be expected to score at the top of the scale for *all* these qualities, but I would make an attempt to assess them all, and to get an indication of the applicant's potential for development in those areas in which he or she scored less highly.

The other part of training involves the study of a number of social science subjects – psychology, sociology, social policy and law – and this requires the capacity for clear thinking and good self-expression. The academic part of social work courses is, of course, not simply a matter of cramming people full of theories, or equipping them with technical skills. It is also an attempt to sharpen up their abilities to think and argue clearly (since they will have to be able to 'think on their feet' in a variety of taxing situations including case conferences with other formidable professionals), and to express themselves accurately in written reports (for example, in court reports, which may be crucial in determining a client's future).

The pathway leading into social work and through training is changing. As I have indicated, the first training courses to be established eventually consolidated together as the Certificate of Qualification in Social Work (CQSW), were predominantly aimed at fieldworkers. Only a very small proportion of residential workers received training, and few specialist courses for them were established. With this in mind, a new kind of training, the Certificate in Social Service (CSS), was set up in the mid-1970s. Whereas the CQSW had been a college- or university-based course, often right away from the student's previous employment, and sometimes taking applicants from outside social work, the CSS (which was mainly but not exclusively for residential workers) embodied a much larger element of 'on the job' trainng.

Since then a number of factors have influenced the training scene. Firstly, financial stringency has limited the expansion of training, so that the CSS, although it has proved popular with employers in the local authorities, has not grown as rapidly as hoped. Secondly, the number of new fieldwork posts for CQSW holders has declined, and both government and employers are increasingly concerned to shift the emphasis of training towards the residential sector. Thirdly, there is understandable concern that the two separate kinds of training are on parallel lines, but the qualifications are not interchangeable, which seems to consolidate differentials of status and pay between field and residential workers (and the increasing number of day-care workers, who also tend to do CSS courses). Thus, ways are being urgently sought both to increase training opportunities in the residential and day-care sector, and to clarify the relationship between the two kinds of training, possibly by integrating them into a 'modular' system.

It is generally recognized that the CQSW, in common with other college-based training courses (such as teacher-training), places much emphasis on a good *general* education for aspiring social workers, on encouraging them to think widely and deeply about social problems. It is less designed to train them for the specifics of any particular post, partly because students do not necessarily know what job they will be doing at the end of the course, and have to be prepared for a number of possible options. Employers find this rather unsatisfactory, and tend to prefer the 'on the job' style of the CSS.

It is difficult to predict the future of training, except to say that it will focus increasingly on residential work and day-care. Already, few entrants into social work are able to get experience of fieldwork before training; but courses still tend to prefer to take people with some experience of practice. Hence a large proportion of students on CQSW courses have done some residential work, and residential homes and hostels are staffed to a considerable extent by young people who are getting experience prior to training. This situation invites the possibility of radical new methods of training, aimed at reaching a number of staff in the same institutions – for instance, through Open University courses, or some other form of 'distance teaching'.

However this may be, it is likely that the pathway into

social work will lie in future, especially for younger applicants, through residential or day-care work. This is a particularly demanding way of testing motivation and resilience. The best in residential care offers an inspiring opportunity to focus attention on very needy people in a much more intense and personal way than fieldwork can ever allow. It enables the worker to get to know the client in a more total and rounded way, and for them to share in much more of each other's lives. The worst in residential care involves inexperienced workers in situations and regimes over which they have little control. It absorbs them into systems which are relatively inflexible, and which may entail methods of dealing with residents which are quite contrary to the worker's standards and beliefs, but which he can find no immediate way of changing. Because residential establishments are often the 'last resorts', because they tend to be understaffed and sometimes very isolated, they can become intense hothouses for all the most difficult dilemmas described in this book. The would-be social worker may well have to endure a period of extreme discomfort and doubt as part of the process leading up to the qualification, and before discovering a more fulfilling role.

On the other hand, residential work does allow for a greater degree of specialization than fieldwork. The entrant into social work who has a strong desire to help deprived children, the mentally handicapped or the elderly can choose to work exclusively with these groups in residential homes or day centres, whereas the fieldworker usually has to be more of an all-rounder. In this way, the residential worker may be able to tap his or her motivation more directly in the work, and so find it more satisfying.

Further Reading

For someone who is approaching the literature on social work for the first time, a word of warning is in order. I have tried in this book to convey my conviction that social work is an exciting, challenging, occasionally even inspiring activity. Unfortunately, none of these adjectives can be applied to the vast majority of the texts on the subject which have been published.

There are several reasons for this. The first is a regrettable attempt, from the first beginnings of practice, to organize, classify and codify methods in such a way as to give it the appearance of a scientific discipline, mainly modelled on medicine. In the process of trying to do this, writers have squeezed the life out of it, and in particular smothered the real dilemmas which are at its core, and which have been the central topics of this book.

Secondly, the professional literature first available came mainly from the United States, and was couched largely in the peculiarly bowdlerized and coy language of expurgated Freudianism which characterized its practice in the private sector there, and which was so devastatingly attacked by Barbara Wootton in her *Social Science and the Social Pathology* (Allen & Unwin, 1960). American literature is now infinitely more diverse and interesting, but still often misleading as far as British problems and practices are concerned. But in the meanwhile it set a pattern of British writing on the professional aspects of practice which has still not entirely been broken.

Thirdly, the majority of the literature is written by academics, many of whom are no longer in practice, and some of whom have forgotten what it was like to practise. As in other academic disciplines, the link between publications and promotion calls forth a stream of articles and books which add little to true wisdom or practical expertise. Meanwhile, those with real experience and new ideas often lack the time and skill to write about them. Hence there is a danger of books being written by people with nothing to say, and those with something to say being unable to write.

For newcomers who really want to find out what it is like to be a social worker, it is perhaps best to start with fairly specialized and detailed accounts by practitioners of their corners of the work; even if these are unrepresentative of the overall picture, they often convey a more realistic flavour than the much more generalized impressions of the academic writers. For instance, Jane Sparrow's *Diary of a Delinquent Episode* (Routledge & Kegan Paul, 1976), though an account of residential work in the 1950s, is still a horrifically accurate picture of the worst in work with disturbed girls. Bob Holman's account in *Kids at the Door* (Blackwell Practice of Social Work Series, 1981) of a project working with children and adolescents on a council estate is more uplifting and equally vivid. I am biased in favour of the approach adopted in the Blackwell series, being one of its general editors, but I would also strongly recommend, for the same reasons, Janet Mattinson and Ian Sinclair's *Mate and Stalemate* (1979); Barbara Kahan's *Growing Up in Care* (1979); the collection of essays in *Creative Social Work* (edited by myself and David Brandon, 1979); Gill Lonsdale, Peter Elfer and Rod Ballard's *Children, Grief and Social Work*, (1979); Tom O'Neill's *A Place Called Hope* (1981); Martin Wilkinson's *Children and Divorce* (1981); Nancy Hazel's *A Bridge to Independence* (1981); and John Fitzgerald's *Building New Families* (1982), all in the Blackwell series. A more general book on aspects of practice is my own *Helping in Social Work* (Routledge & Kegan Paul, 1979).

Another source of vivid accounts of the real world of practice is the writings of social scientists who have observed practitioners at work. I have quoted extensively from Carole Satyamurti's *Occupational Survival*, and would recommend people to read it in full for an account of the complexities and awfulnesses of generic social work. But others have looked at particular aspects of practice equally usefully. For instance, on juvenile delinquency, Howard Parker, Maggie Casburn and David Turnbull's *Receiving Juvenile Justice* (Blackwell, 1981) is lively and challenging. It is usefully complemented, from an entirely different perspective by Owen Gill's *Luke Street*, (Macmillan, 1977).

Spencer Millham, Roger Bullock and Paul Cherrett's *After Grace – Teeth* (Chaucer, 1975) is still worth reading for its account of the approved school system. Rather more theoretical, but also important and occasionally memorable are Roy King, Norma Raynes and Jack Tizard's *Patterns of Residential Care* (Routledge & Kegan Paul, 1971) on mentally handicapped children; and E. J. Miller and G. V. Gwynne's *A Life Apart* (Tavistock, 1972) on homes for the severely physically handicapped. Also recommended are Owen Gill and Barbara Jackson's *Adoption and Race* (Batsford, 1983); and Mervyn Murch's *Justice and Welfare in Divorce* (Sweet & Maxwell, 1980).

Studies of the development of policy can throw light on practice, as I have tried to argue in much of this book. For child care policy I recommend Jean Packman's *The Child's Generation* (Blackwell & Robertson, second edition, 1982). A new book by her on admissions to care will be published in 1984. David Thorpe, *et al.*'s *Out of Care* (Allen & Unwin, 1980), is provocative and interesting about policy over delinquency, as is Spencer Millham, Roger Bullock and Ken Hosie's *Locking Up Children* (Saxon House, 1978). For probation, David Haxby's *Probation: A Changing Service* is probably the best of a rather dull bunch.

In mental health, Kathleen Jones's *Mental Health and Social Policy* (Routledge & Kegan Paul, 1960) is very thorough, and Philip Bean's *Compulsory Admissions to Mental Hospitals* (Wiley, 1980) is stimulating, even though I believe he has barked up the wrong trees. On the elderly, and mentally handicapped children, see R. M. Moroney's *The Family and the State* (Longman, 1976).

Political accounts of social work tend to be couched in heavily Marxist terms, unless (as in Colin Brewer and June Lait's *Can Social Work Survive?*, Temple Smith, 1980) they are equally ideologically committed to the hard right. A recent book which attempts to draw political lessons from practice is *The Political Dimensions of Social Work*, which I edited with Nigel Parton, (Blackwell Practice of Social Work Series, 1983).

Of the Marxist texts, Paul Corrigan and Peter Leonard's *Social Work Practice under Capitalism* (Macmillan, 1978) and S. Bolger, P. Corrigan, J. Docking and N. Frost's *Towards Socialist Welfare Work* (Macmillan, 1981) are the best known. See also on probation, H. Walker and D. Beaumont's *Probation Work: Critical Theory and Practice* (Blackwell, 1981).

Index

adolescents, 23, 24–5, 118
adoption, 18, 144–5
almoners, 71, 75
almsgiving, 40
Attlee, Clement, 42, 45, 118, 145
Austen, Jane, 39–40
Australia, 6, 133
automation, 23, 133
Axline, Virginia, 52–5

Barclay Committee, 99, 136–42
Barnardo's, 12
Belgium, 117–8
Bentham, Jeremy, 184–5
bereavement, 60
Beveridge, Lord, 67, 73, 75, 76, 112
Bismarck, Prince Otto von, 113–4
Bleak House, 35–7, 39
British Agencies for Adoption and Fostering, 144–5
Britton, Bruce, 174–5
Brixton, 23, 46
'burn-out', 16, 62, 153
Butler, Josephine, 32

capitalist production, 43, 111–2, 133, 141–2, 146–8

Carpenter, Mary, 32
Case Con, 57
Certificate of Qualification in Social Work, 187–9
Certificate in Social Service, 143, 187–9
charities, 31–41, 46, 115
Charity Organization Society, 40
child abuse, 6, 7, 11, 20–1, 67–71, 94–6, 134, 136, 175, 183–4
child care, 10, 11, 17–18, 19, 23, 68–80, 90–1, 94–6, 98–100, 102, 115, 143–6, 144–5, 156
Child Guidance Clinics, 55, 71, 81, 88
Children's departments, 68–74, 76–7, 78, 79–80, 82, 84, 87–8
children's homes, 8, 11, 19, 73–4, 78, 83, 90, 103, 117–18, 178
Clark, Brian, 58–60
class conflict, 43, 45–6, 57, 114, 147
Colwell, Maria, 21, 94–6
Community Development Projects, 122
community work, 12, 13, 42, 138–42, 178–81

compulsory powers, 17–18, 60, 62, 97–8, 126–8, 134, 166
Conservative Party, 111, 125–6, 147–8
Cooper, Mike, 139
Crane, Miss, 47
crime, 31, 55, 123–30
criminal justice system, 123–7
Curtis Committee, 68, 70–4, 78, 93, 115
Cyrenians, 12

Dalton, Hugh, 45
Davies, Martin, 127
day care, 4, 8, 10, 11, 92, 143, 183, 188–9
Defoe, Daniel, 34–5
delinquency, 6, 7, 11, 22, 23, 85, 87, 118, 125–6, 134, 136, 165–8, 183–4
Dharamsi, Fatma, 27
Dibs, 52–5
Dickens, Charles, 35–9
divorce, 6, 12
  and conciliation, 177, 184
Drake, Frances, 77
Dysart, Martin, 58

economics, 1, 43, 45, 112, 122, 132–4, 146–8, 181–4
  planning, 77
  growth, 86–7
education, 2, 6, 7, 11, 31, 54, 72, 78, 88, 90, 111, 134, 146, 162, 164–8
  welfare, 83, 88
elderly, 4, 6, 10, 17, 20, 73, 79, 83, 84, 90
Eliot, George, 35
empathy, 13–14, 51, 56
employment, 132–4

factory inspectors, 75, 76–7

families, 15, 17, 21–2, 53–5, 91, 136, 144
  centres 183
  problem, 85–6, 103
  and the state, 97–100, 174
  violence, 97, 160–1
  work, 87, 155–6
family therapy, 12
fantasy, 50–63, 82
financial aid, 92
Flanders, Moll, 34–5
foster parents, 68–9, 73–4, 84, 91, 94–5, 117–8
France, 43
Freud, Sigmund, 42–4, 50, 55
Fry, Elizabeth, 32, 35, 37–8

Germany, 43, 112–4, 132
Gingerbread, 18, 99
Gissing, George, 43
Glasgow, 23
Gough, Reginald, 67–9
Green, T. H., 41
Griffiths, Bill, 127
group work, 12, 42, 170–3
Growth Movement, 61–2

Hadley, Professor Roger, 137–8
Hall, Penelope, 110
handicap, 6, 10, 58–9, 79, 83, 85, 87, 163
Hardy, Thomas, 43
Harrison, Ken, 58–60
Hazel, Nancy, 117
health services, 6, 11, 45, 67, 78, 90, 96, 100, 116, 136–7, 146, 162–3, 168–9
Health and Social Security, Department of (DHSS), 12, 76, 86, 96
health visitors, 4
Higgins, Joan, 116
Hill, Octavia, 32, 37, 38, 40

Hobbes, Thomas, 182–3
Hollywood, 56–7
home helps, 4, 8, 10, 83, 88, 92, 100, 103
homelessness, 12, 42, 83, 118, 143–4
Home Office, 12, 70, 76, 82
hospitals, 11, 15, 163
housing, 3, 6, 37–8, 45, 75, 84, 90, 111, 116, 134, 146, 181
immigrants, 21
India, 46–8
industrialization, 32–3, 114, 132–3
intermediate treatment, 12, 183–4

James, Adrian, 127
Japan, 5, 110
Jellyby, Mrs, 35–6
Jordan, Bill, 27
juvenile courts, 87, 125–6, 142

Kahan, Barbara, 76–7
Kennedy, Ian, 163
Kesey, Ken, 58
Keynes, J. M., 112
Konrad, George, 62–3

Labour Party, 45, 86–7, 111–2, 125–6, 134, 146–7
Lane, Homer, 50–1, 55
law-enforcement, 50
Lawrence, D. H., 43
lawyers, 1, 31, 164, 168
Lenin, V. I., 182–3
Liberal Party, 111–3
Longford, Lord, 87

Macadam, Elizabeth, 75–8, 120
McMurphy, Randle P., 58
Manners, Daphne, 47–8

Manpower Services Commission, 143
Mansfield Park, 39–40
Marshall, T. H., 110
Marx, Karl, 23, 42–3, 57, 114, 146–8
Mattinson, Janet, 155–6
Mayer, J. E., 26
medicine, 1, 31, 88, 94, 96, 100, 162–5, 168–73
medical social workers, 87
mental hospitals, 58, 60, 63, 71, 81, 157–60, 168–73, 178
mental illness, 7, 11, 51, 73, 85, 87, 134, 139, 157–60, 168–73
Mill, John Stuart, 41
Millham, Spencer, 131
Monckton, Sir Walter, 67–70, 93
moral issues, 9–10, 26, 31–44, 45–63, 151–61, 163

National Assistance Board, 75, 79, 87
National Children's Bureau, 27
National Children's Homes, 12
negotiation, 121–2, 164, 175–80, 182–4
Neill, A. S., 54–5
New Zealand, 6
Nightingale, Florence, 32
Normanton, 139

occupational therapists, 88, 166
old people's homes, 5, 10, 83, 84, 88, 90, 103–4
O'Neill, Dennis, 67–71, 94–5
O'Neill, Tom, 69, 94–5
Oxfordshire, 76, 85

Packman, Jean, 98–9, 160

Pardiggle, Mrs, 36
parents, 2, 18, 68, 98–9, 144–5,
    165–8
  single, 18, 22, 91, 99, 133,
    146–7
Parker, Howard, 26
Pearson, Geoffrey, 9
pensions, 38
personal relationships, 32–42,
    46–63, 70–1
Peterson, Mr, 25–6
Pinker, Professor Robert, 139
Place of Safety Orders, 17, 98–9,
    139
police, 23, 90, 123, 134–5,
    160–1, 166–7
politics, 1, 7–8, 20–2, 23, 42–4,
    45–6, 50, 61, 81, 86–7,
    109–48, 174–85
Poor Laws, 31–3, 38, 40, 46, 72,
    78–9, 83, 92, 111, 115,
    140–1, 164
poverty, 6, 7, 31–3, 37–8, 40,
    42, 45–6, 57, 85, 86–7, 118
press, 2, 19, 95–6, 99
prevention, 17, 85–7, 138–9,
    141, 169–73
Price, Fanny, 39–40
prisons, 12, 34–5, 37–8, 124–30
probation service, 6, 11–12, 71,
    75, 82, 87–8, 123–30,
    142–3, 152, 160
psychiatric social workers, 71,
    81–2, 87–8, 158, 168–73
psychiatrists, 3, 56, 57–8, 82,
    168–73
psychology, 1, 10, 45, 49–63,
    151–2, 162, 168–73

race relations, 26, 46–8, 57, 119,
    145
Reagan, Ronald, 134

religion, 9, 32–42, 54, 56, 115,
    117
residential homes, 2, 10, 24–5,
    50, 73–4, 79, 83–4, 87, 90,
    92, 152–5, 188–9
residential social work, 2, 10,
    24–6, 42, 51, 71, 83, 90,
    101, 103, 143, 152–3, 160,
    168, 187–8
Rimlinger, G. V., 114
Ruskin, John, 38
Russia, 113–4

Sabel, Brian, 146, 178–80
Sainsbury, Eric, 27
Salvation Army, 38
Satyamurti, Carole, 27, 89–92,
    101–5, 120
Scandinavia, 6, 112
Scotland, 6, 10, 88, 142
Scott, Paul, 46–8
Seebohm Committee, 88–9, 142
sex, 43, 47–9, 50
Shaffer, Peter, 58
Smith, Dr Southwood, 38
social democracy, 84, 132–4
social insurance, *see* social security
social policy, 109–47
social security, 5, 67, 79, 90, 97,
    113–4, 116, 135
social services departments,
    10–11, 17–18, 20–1, 73,
    88–105, 120, 134–43, 146,
    155–6
socialism, 42–4, 49, 112, 174–5
sociology, 1, 10, 47, 60, 119, 162
South Africa, 46, 118
strikes, 16, 120, 129
Stroud, John, 82–3
Summerson, Esther, 35–7
supplementary benefits, 3, 17,
    87, 91–2, 102

Sweden, 116, 118

Thatcher, Margaret, 126, 134
therapy, 50–63
trade unions, 16, 113, 120, 133,
    145, 174
training, 55, 57, 71–2, 75–6, 78,
    81, 83, 86, 119, 129, 140,
    143, 152, 160, 174, 185–9
Tresall, Robert, 43
Trilling, Lionel, 40

unemployment, 3, 7, 22, 45, 77,
    91, 111, 132–4, 143–8, 181
    benefit, 112
USA, 6, 42, 51, 61, 75, 110, 112,
    116, 119, 133, 145, 178

voluntary organizations, 5, 6,
    12, 42, 46, 67, 71, 103, 116,
    138

volunteers, 5

Webb, Sidney and Beatrice, 72,
    111
welfare services, 75, 79, 83–6, 88
Williams Report, 83
women, 43
    feminist, 57
    psychiatric problems of,
        169–70
    in social work, 32–42, 76–7,
        78, 103
    suffrage, 38
    and violence, 160–1

Younghusband Report, 86

Zola, Emile, 43